ZIGGY
GOES FOR BROKE

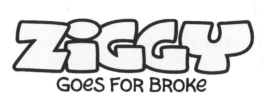

Recent *Ziggy* Books

Ziggy Hot Off the Presses
Ziggy Comes Up Short
Ziggy's Friends for Life
Ziggy on Parade
Ziggy's Gift
Character Matters
Ziggy Goes Hollywood
The Zen of Ziggy
Get Ziggy with It
Ziggy's Divine Comedy

Treasuries

A Little Character Goes a Long Way
The First 25 Years Are the Hardest!
Ziggy's Star Performances

GOES FOR BROKE

A Cartoon Collection

by Tom Wilson

Andrews McMeel
Publishing, LLC

Kansas City · Sydney · London

Ziggy is distributed by Universal Uclick.

Ziggy Goes for Broke copyright © 2010 by Ziggy and Friends, Inc.
All rights reserved. Printed in China. No part of this book may be used
or reproduced in any manner whatsoever without written permission
except in the case of reprints in the context of reviews. For information,
write Andrews McMeel Publishing, LLC, an Andrews McMeel Universal
company, 1130 Walnut Street, Kansas City, Missouri 64106.

ISBN-13: 978-0-7407-9153-6
ISBN-10: 0-7407-9153-2

Library of Congress Control Number: 2009939466

10 11 12 13 14 WKT 10 9 8 7 6 5 4 3 2 1

www.andrewsmcmeel.com

—— **ATTENTION: SCHOOLS AND BUSINESSES** ——

Andrews McMeel books are available at quantity discounts with bulk pur-
chase for educational, business, or sales promotional use. For information,
please write to: Special Sales Department, Andrews McMeel Publishing, LLC,
1130 Walnut Street, Kansas City, Missouri 64106.

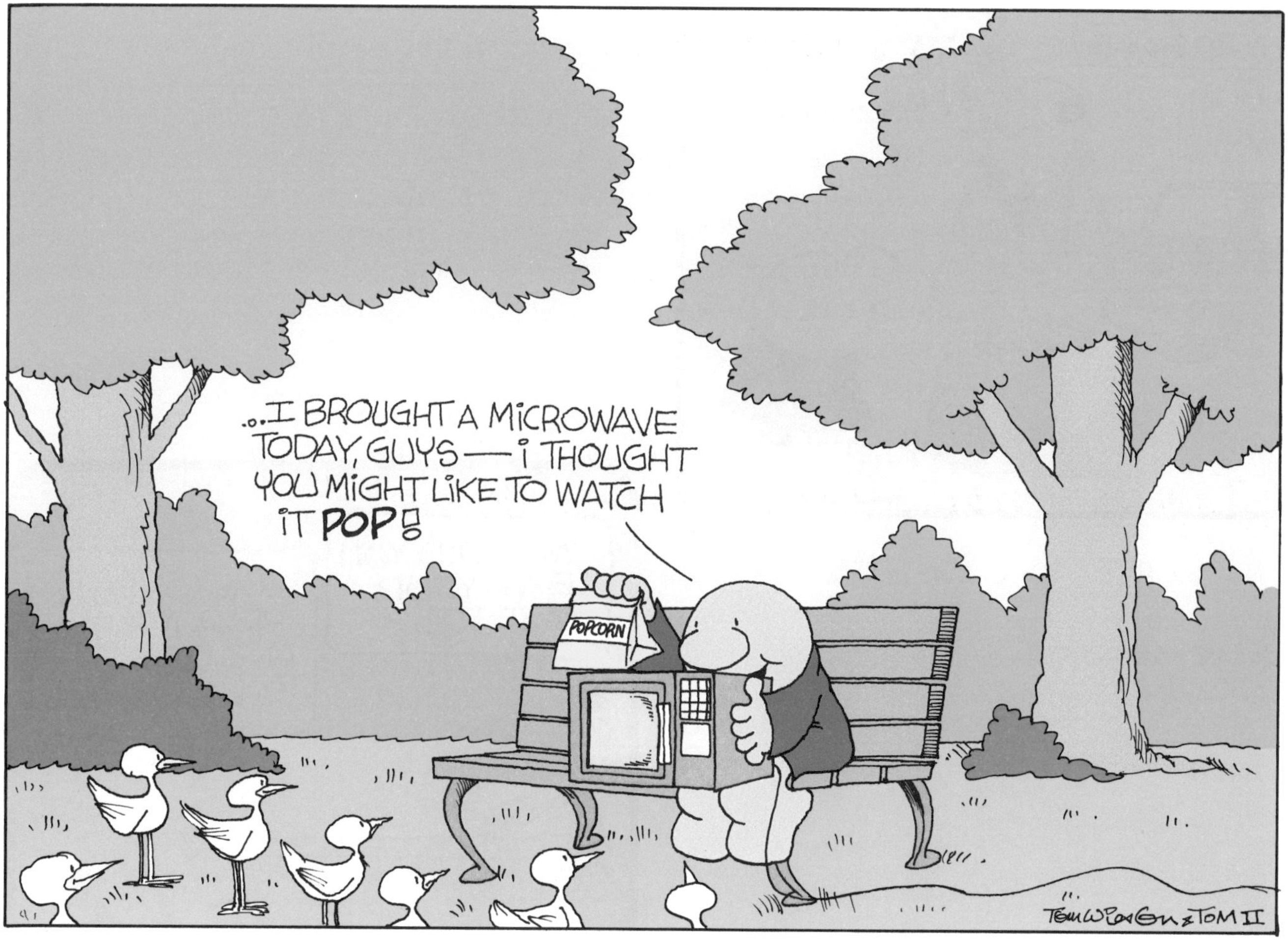

...I BROUGHT A MICROWAVE TODAY, GUYS — I THOUGHT YOU MIGHT LIKE TO WATCH IT POP!!
POPCORN

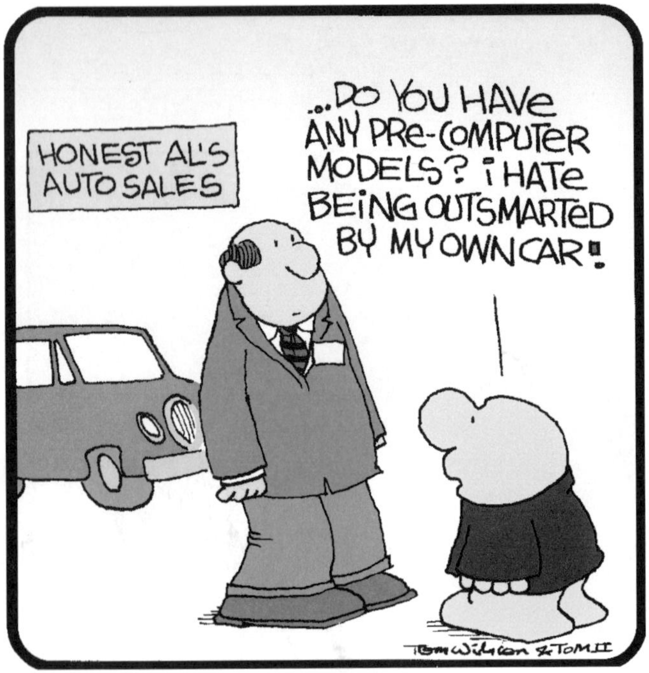

HONEST AL'S AUTO SALES
...DO YOU HAVE ANY PRE-COMPUTER MODELS? I HATE BEING OUTSMARTED BY MY OWN CAR!
Tom Wilson & TOM II

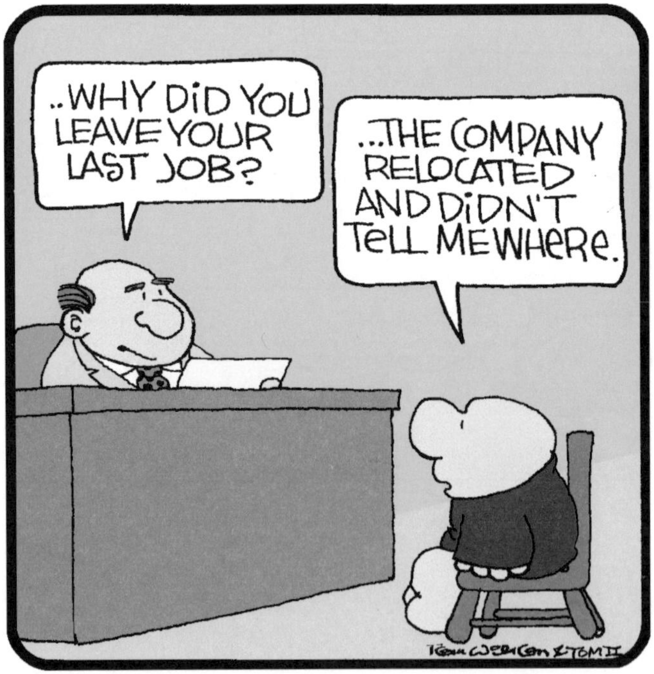

..WHY DID YOU LEAVE YOUR LAST JOB?
...THE COMPANY RELOCATED AND DIDN'T TELL ME WHERE.
Tom Wilson & TOM II

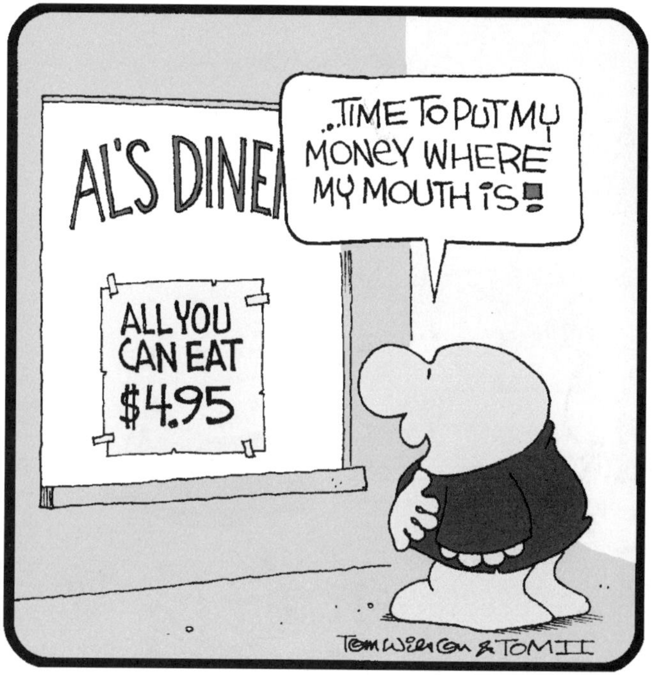
AL'S DINER
ALL YOU CAN EAT $4.95
..TIME TO PUT MY MONEY WHERE MY MOUTH IS!!
TOM WILSON & TOM II

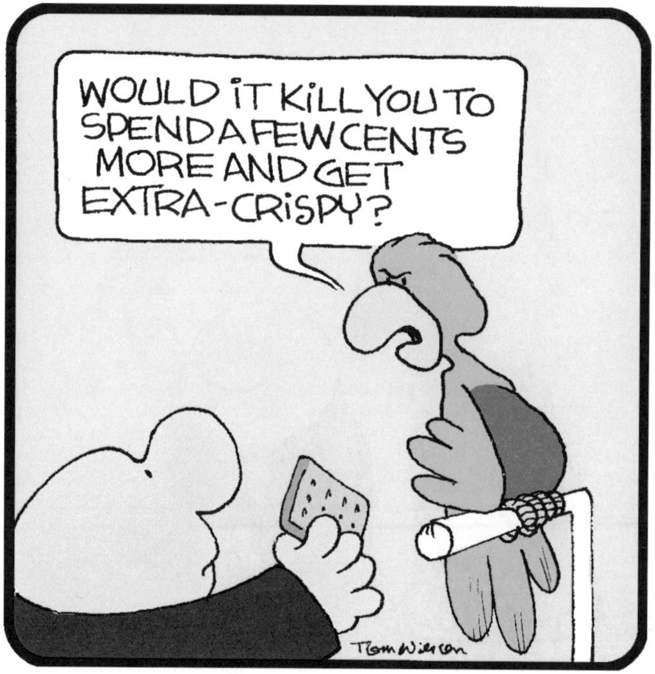
WOULD IT KILL YOU TO SPEND A FEW CENTS MORE AND GET EXTRA-CRISPY?
TOM WILSON

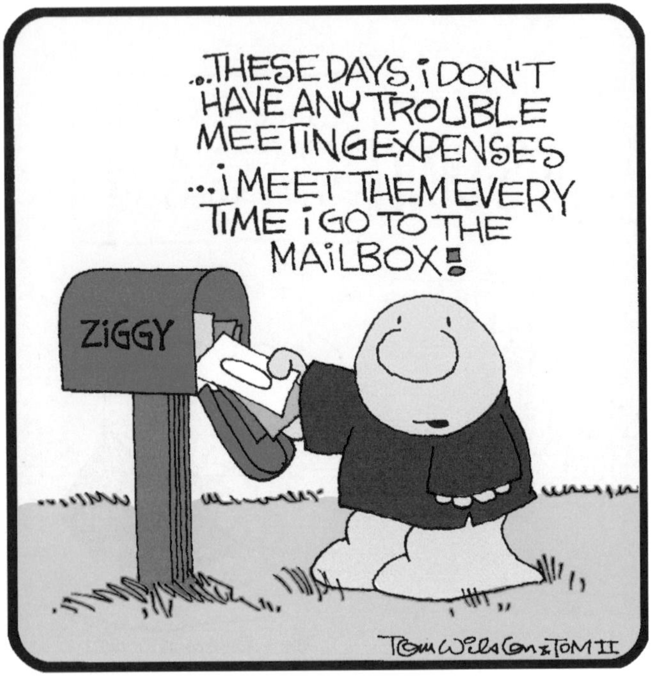
..THESE DAYS, i DON'T HAVE ANY TROUBLE MEETING EXPENSES ...i MEET THEM EVERY TIME i GO TO THE MAiLBOX!
ZiGGY
TOM WILSON & TOM II

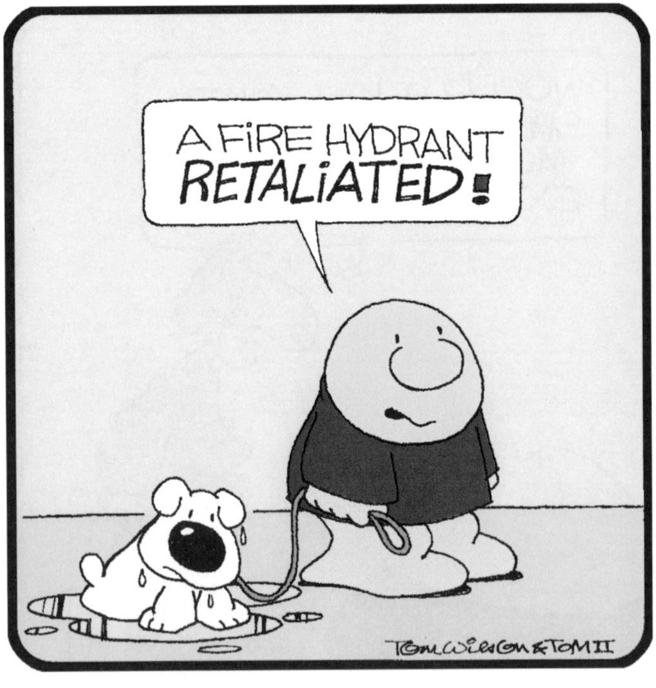
A FiRE HYDRANT RETALiATED!
TOM WILSON & TOM II

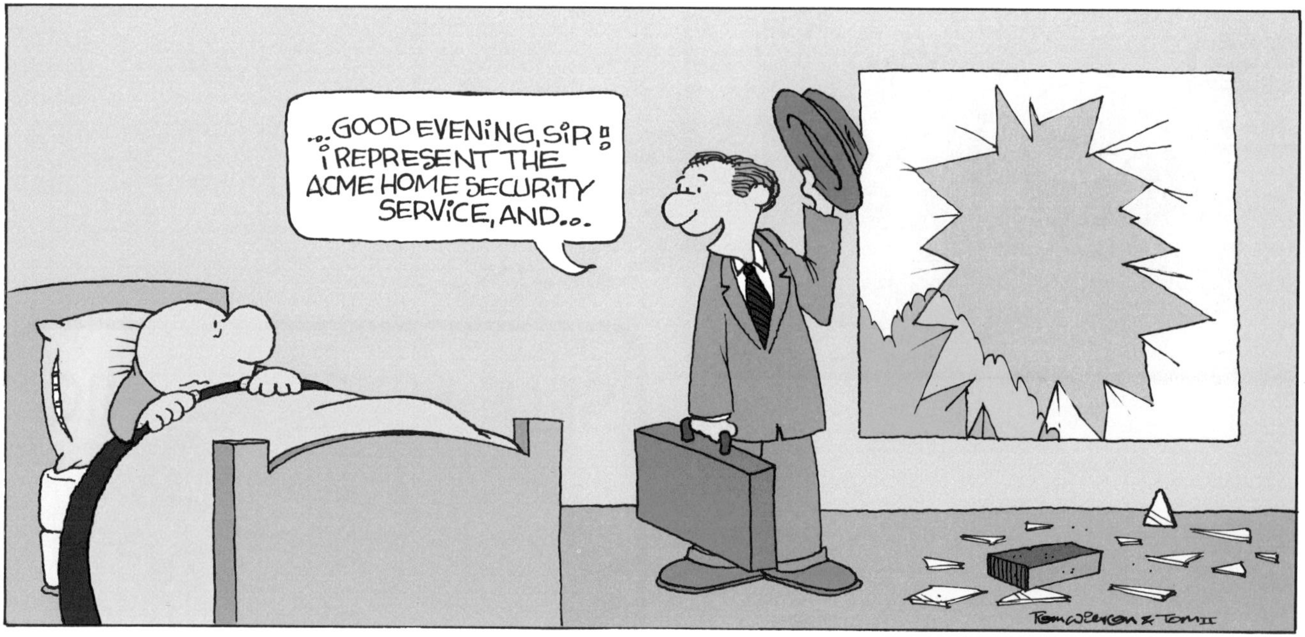
...GOOD EVENING, SIR! I REPRESENT THE ACME HOME SECURITY SERVICE, AND...
TOM WILSON & TOM II

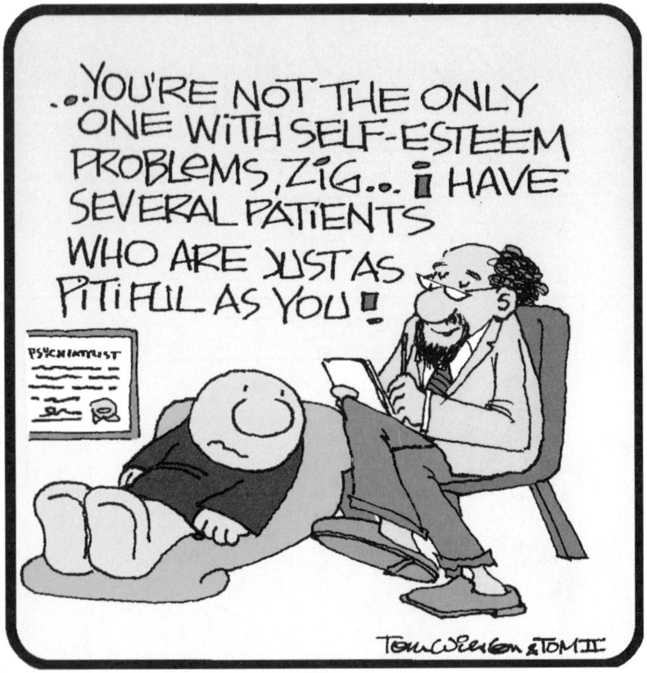
..YOU'RE NOT THE ONLY ONE WITH SELF-ESTEEM PROBLEMS, ZIG.. I HAVE SEVERAL PATIENTS WHO ARE JUST AS PITIFUL AS YOU!
PSYCHIATRIST
Tom Wilson & TOM II

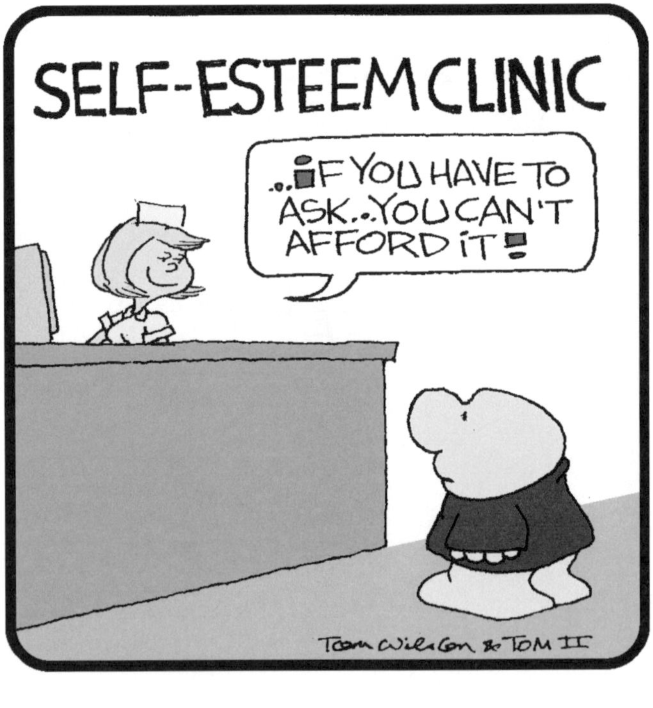
SELF-ESTEEM CLINIC
..IF YOU HAVE TO ASK..YOU CAN'T AFFORD IT!
Tom Wilson & TOM II

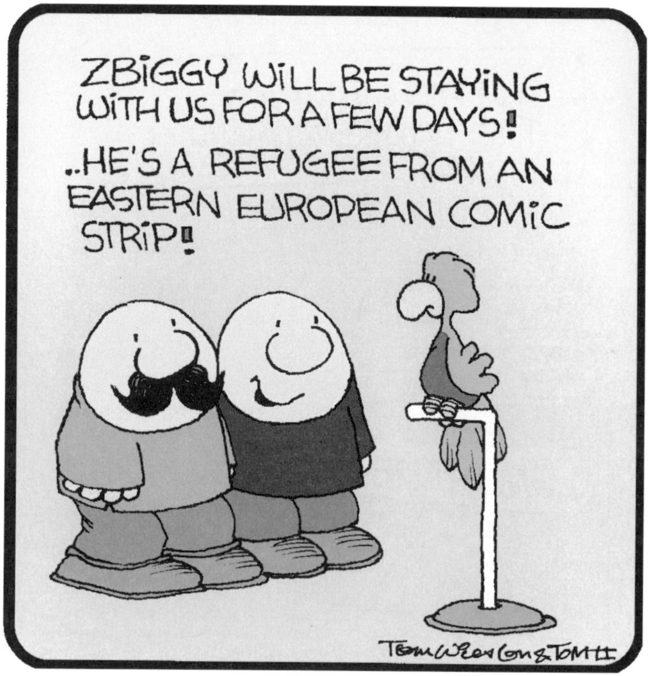
ZBIGGY WILL BE STAYING WITH US FOR A FEW DAYS!
..HE'S A REFUGEE FROM AN EASTERN EUROPEAN COMIC STRIP!
TOM WILSON & TOM II

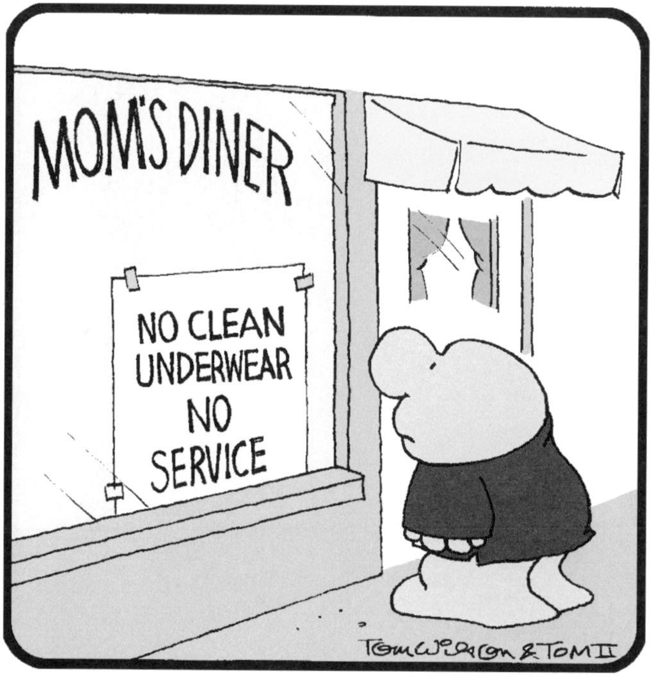
MOM'S DINER
NO CLEAN UNDERWEAR NO SERVICE
TOM WILSON & TOM II

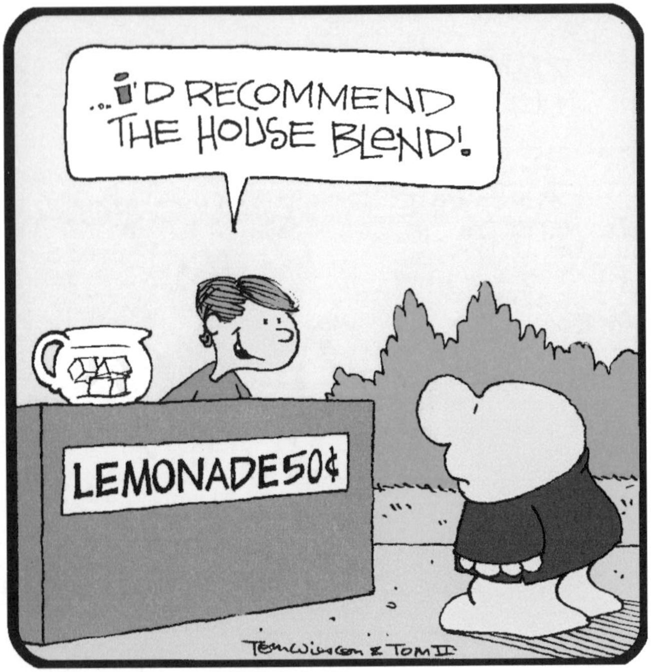
..I'D RECOMMEND THE HOUSE BLEND!
LEMONADE 50¢

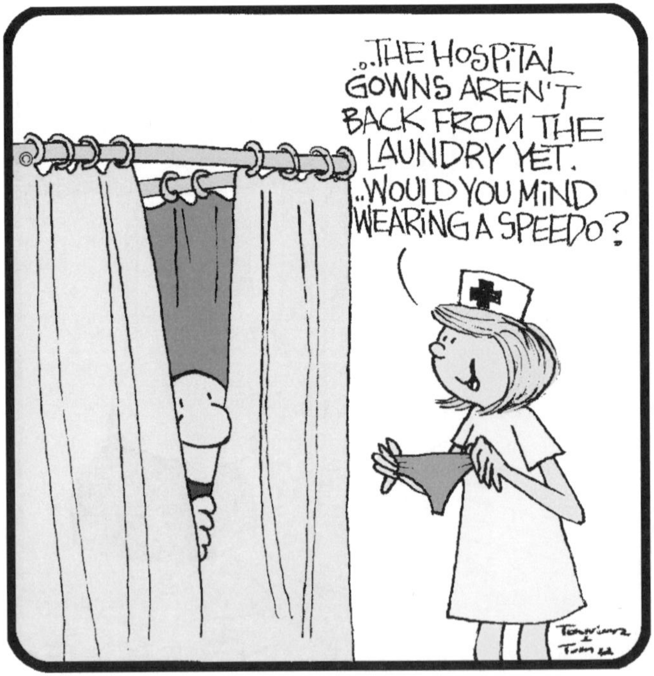
..THE HOSPITAL GOWNS AREN'T BACK FROM THE LAUNDRY YET. ..WOULD YOU MIND WEARING A SPEEDO?

MEN'S ROOM
RETURNS
TAKE A NUMBER
NUMBER THREE!
437
...IF GETTING AHEAD IN LIFE IS YOUR AIM..
LIFE
...THEN SIMPLY SHOWING UP IS THE MAIN PART OF THE GAME!!
-FOR OLIVIA W/THANKS!
TOM WILSON & TOM II

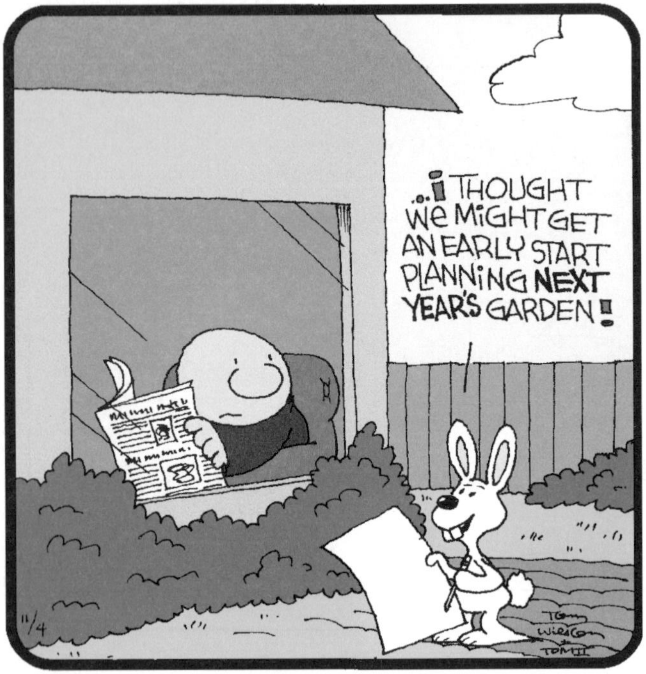
..I THOUGHT WE MIGHT GET AN EARLY START PLANNING NEXT YEAR'S GARDEN!

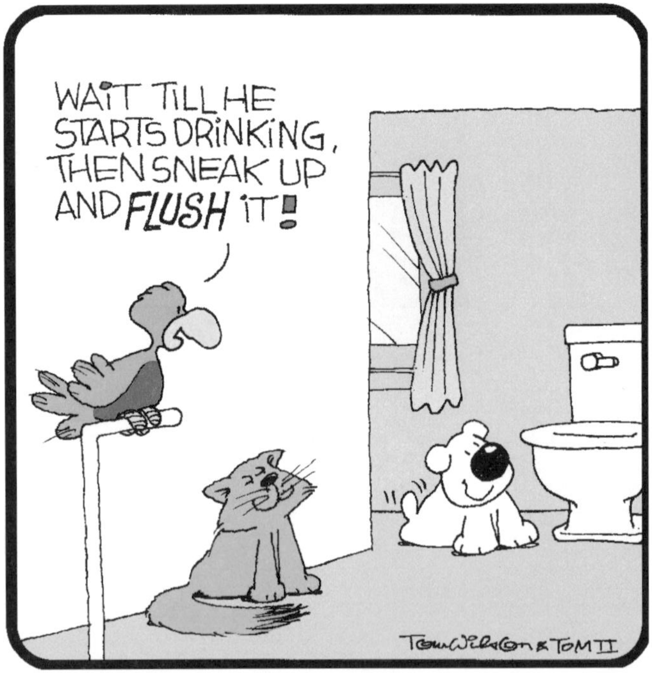
WAIT TILL HE STARTS DRINKING, THEN SNEAK UP AND FLUSH IT!

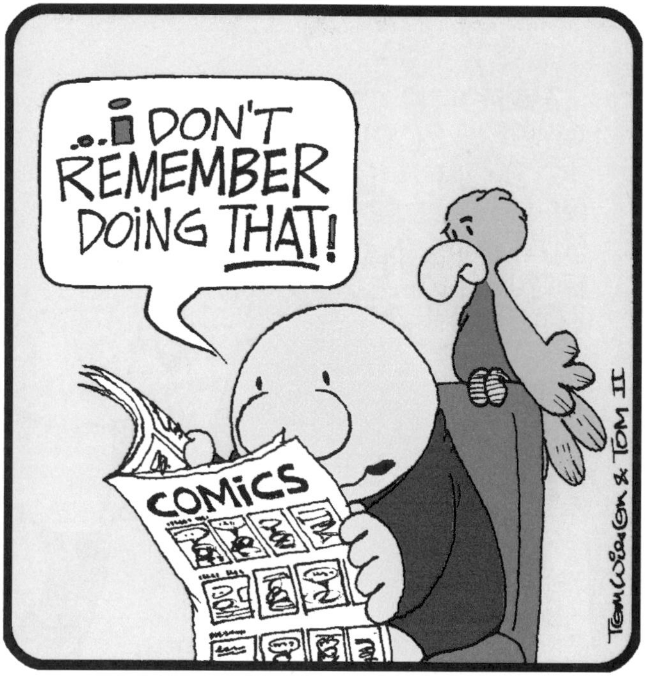
...i DON'T REMEMBER DOING THAT!
COMICS
TOM WILSON & TOM II

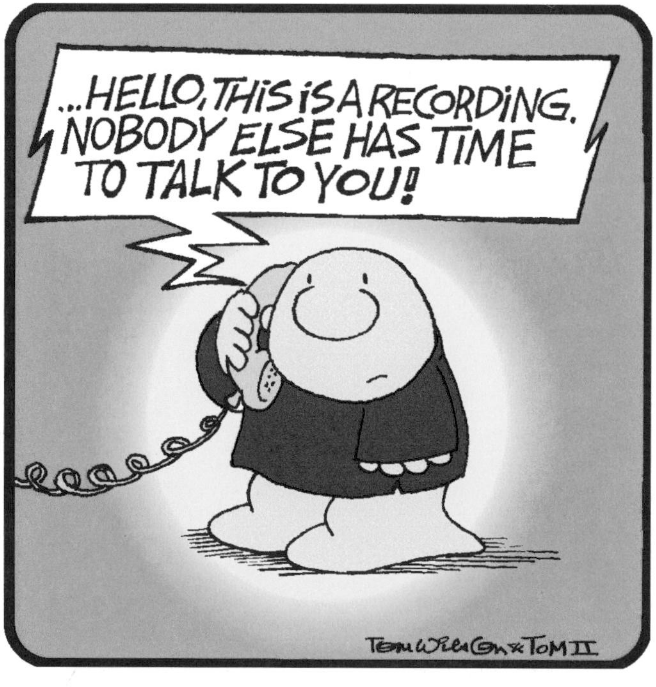
...HELLO, THIS IS A RECORDING. NOBODY ELSE HAS TIME TO TALK TO YOU!
TOM WILSON & TOM II

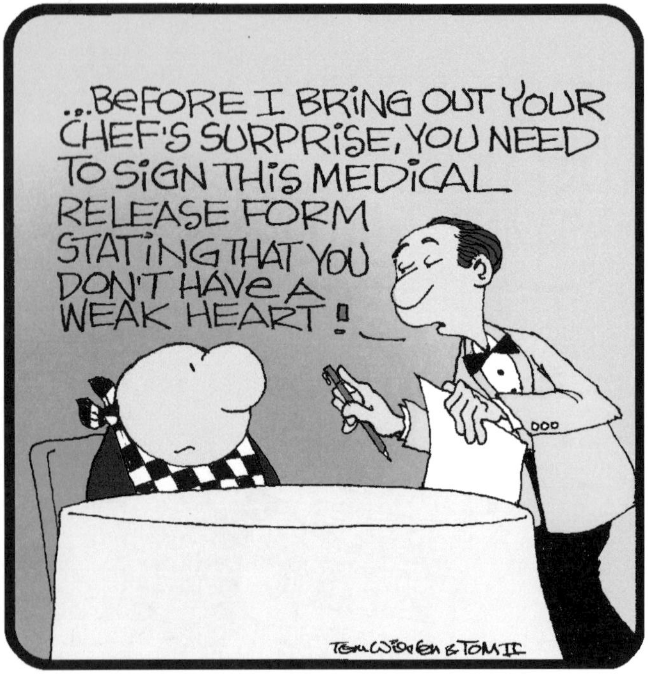
...BEFORE I BRING OUT YOUR CHEF'S SURPRISE, YOU NEED TO SIGN THIS MEDICAL RELEASE FORM STATING THAT YOU DON'T HAVE A WEAK HEART!
TOM WILSON & TOM II

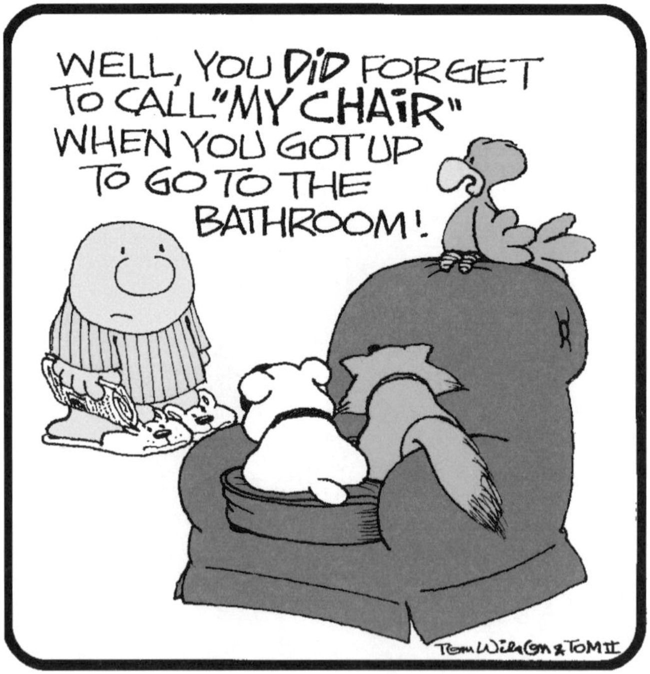
WELL, YOU DID FORGET TO CALL "MY CHAIR" WHEN YOU GOT UP TO GO TO THE BATHROOM!
TOM WILSON & TOM II

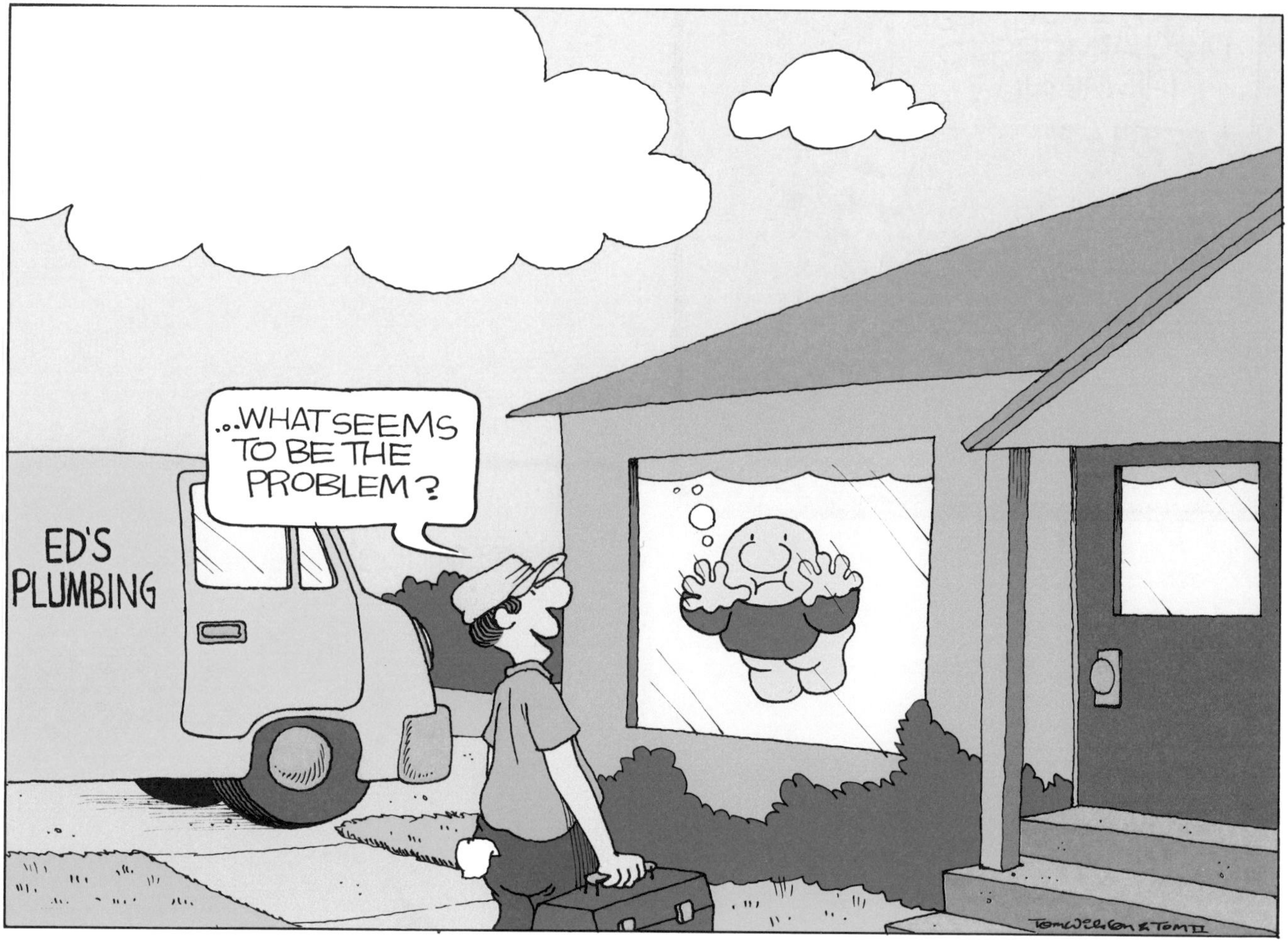
...WHAT SEEMS TO BE THE PROBLEM?
ED'S PLUMBING
TOM WILSON & TOM II

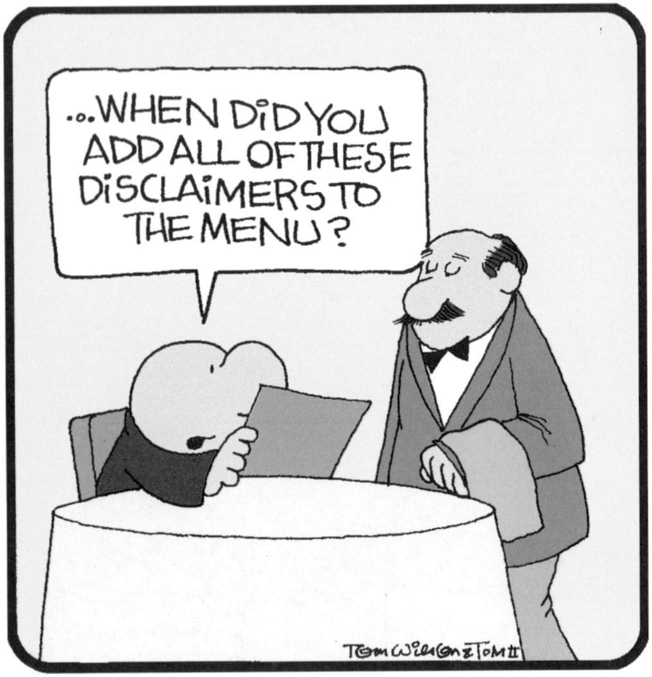
...WHEN DID YOU ADD ALL OF THESE DISCLAIMERS TO THE MENU?
TOM WILSON & TOM II

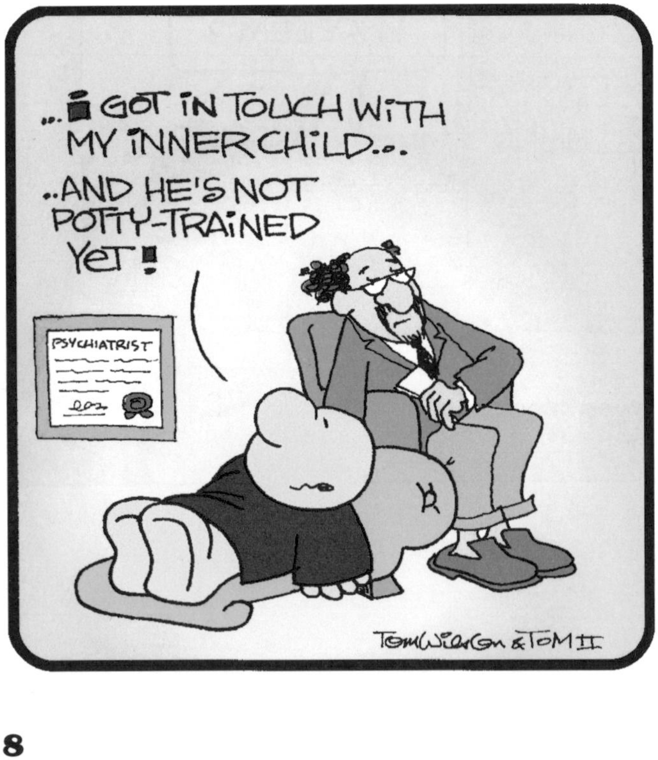
...I GOT IN TOUCH WITH MY INNER CHILD...
..AND HE'S NOT POTTY-TRAINED YET!
PSYCHIATRIST
TOM WILSON & TOM II

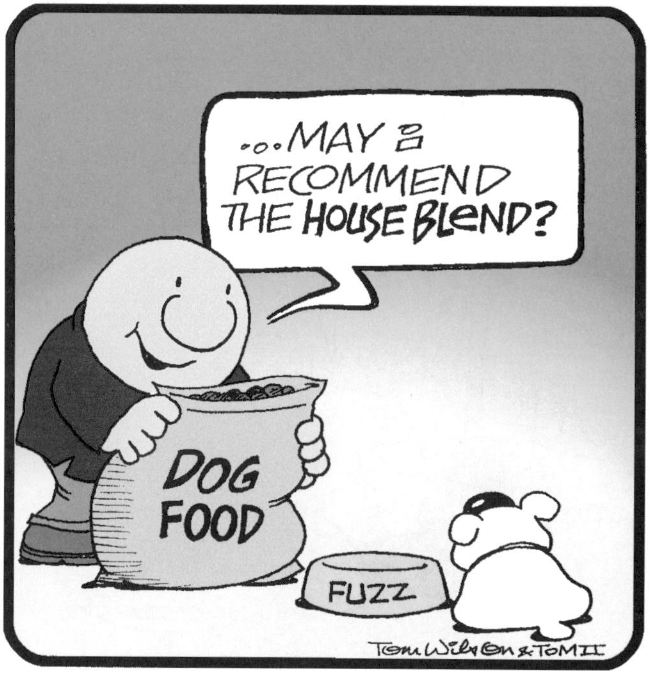
...MAY I
RECOMMEND
THE HOUSE BLEND?
DOG
FOOD
FUZZ
TOM WILSON & TOM II

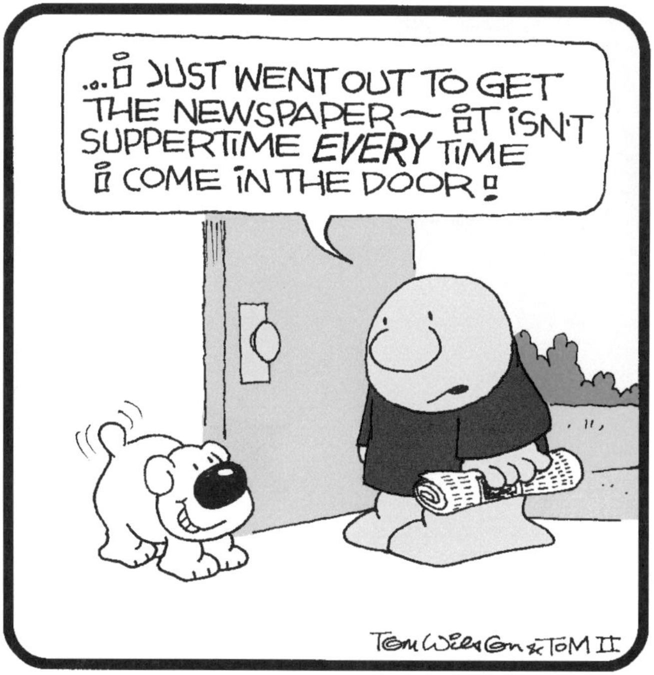
...I JUST WENT OUT TO GET THE NEWSPAPER ~ IT ISN'T SUPPERTIME EVERY TIME I COME IN THE DOOR!
TOM WILSON & TOM II

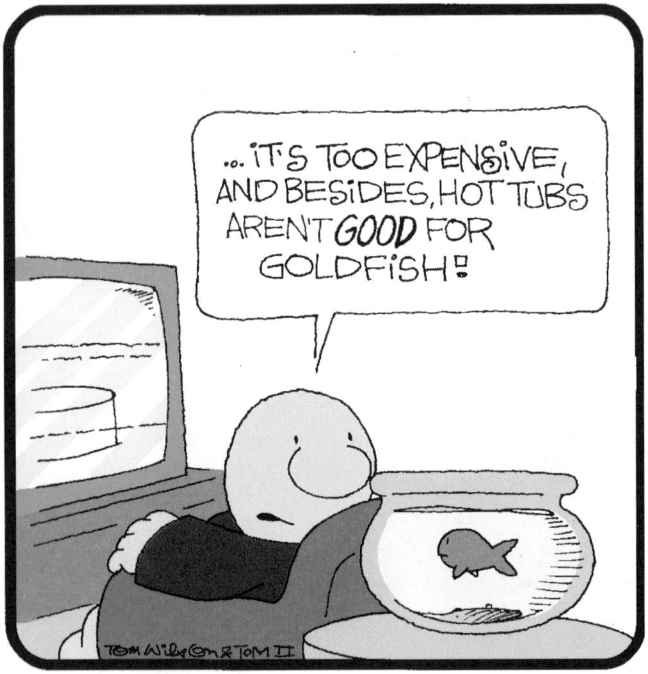
...IT'S TOO EXPENSIVE, AND BESIDES, HOT TUBS AREN'T GOOD FOR GOLDFISH!
TOM WILSON & TOM II

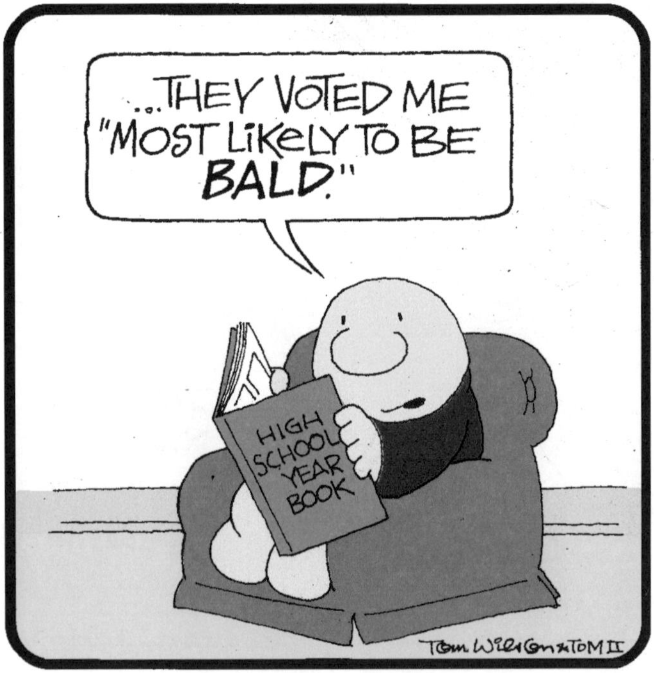
...THEY VOTED ME "MOST LIKELY TO BE BALD."
HIGH SCHOOL YEAR BOOK
TOM WILSON & TOM II

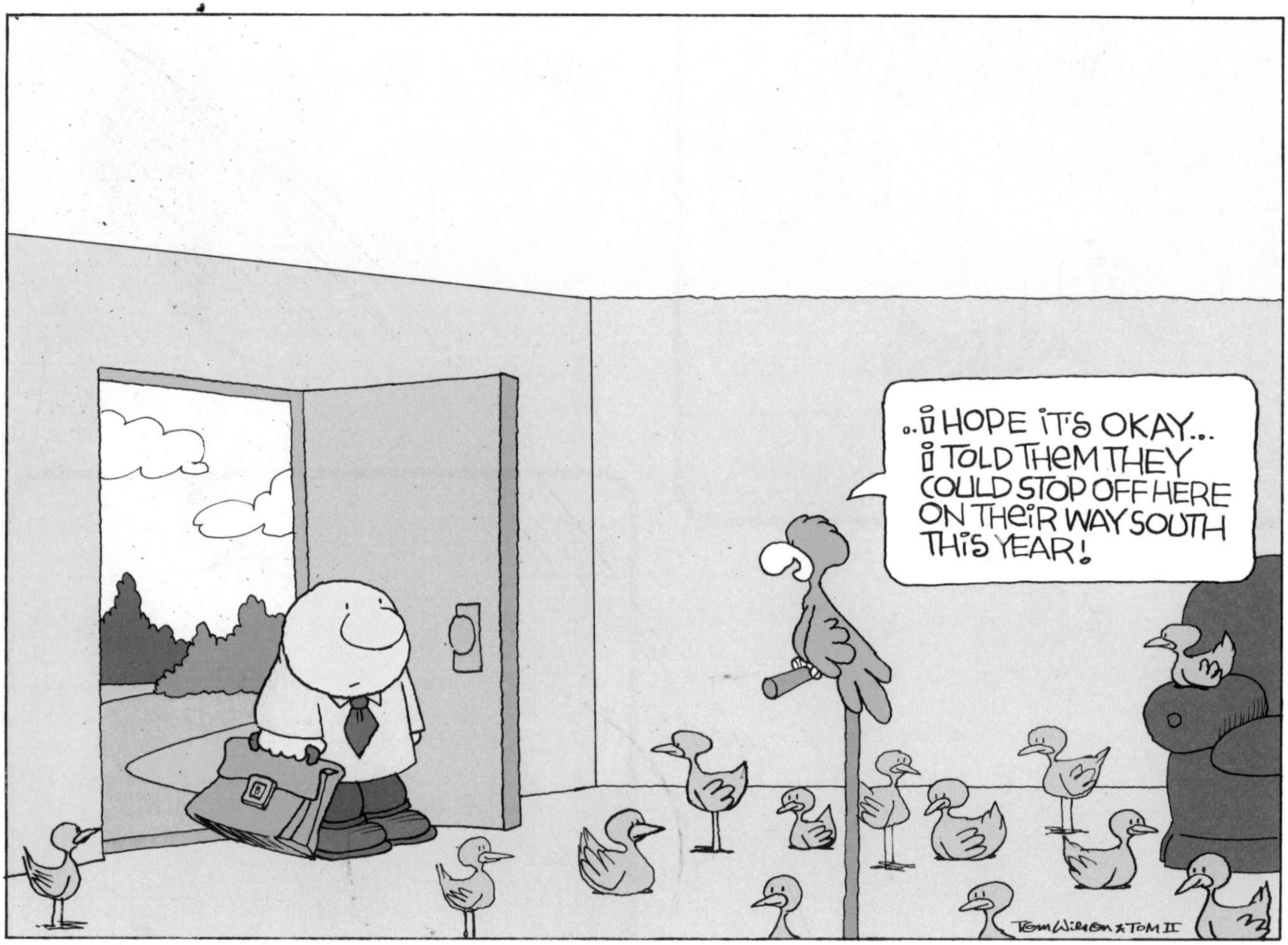
..I HOPE IT'S OKAY... I TOLD THEM THEY COULD STOP OFF HERE ON THEIR WAY SOUTH THIS YEAR!
TOM WILSON & TOM II

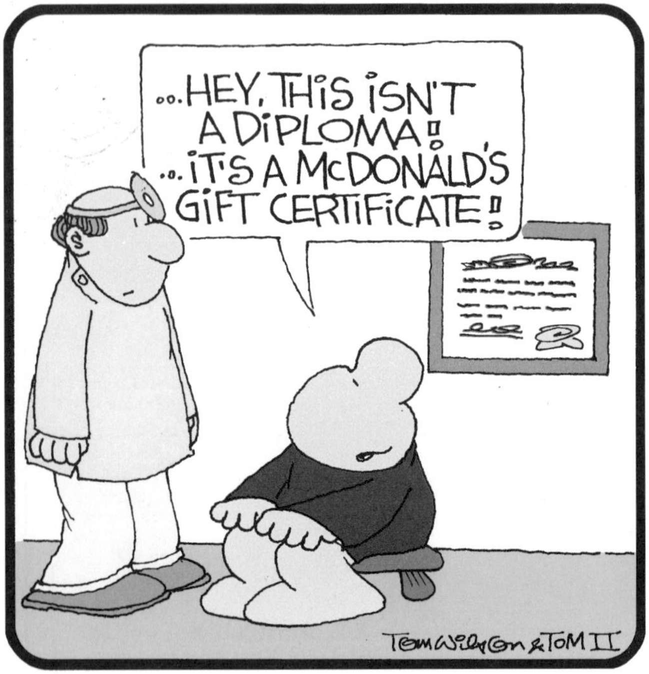
...HEY, THIS ISN'T A DIPLOMA!
...IT'S A McDONALD'S GIFT CERTIFICATE!
TOM WILSON & TOM II

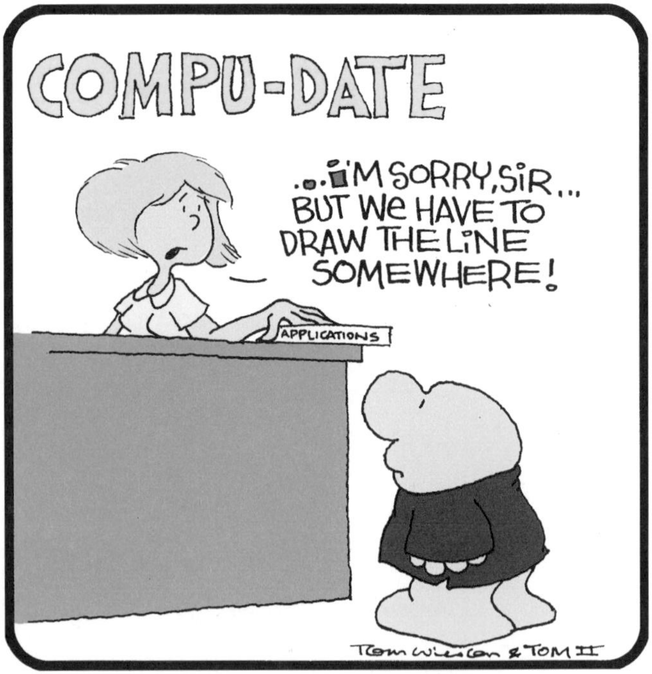
COMPU-DATE
...I'M SORRY, SIR... BUT WE HAVE TO DRAW THE LINE SOMEWHERE!
APPLICATIONS
TOM WILSON & TOM II

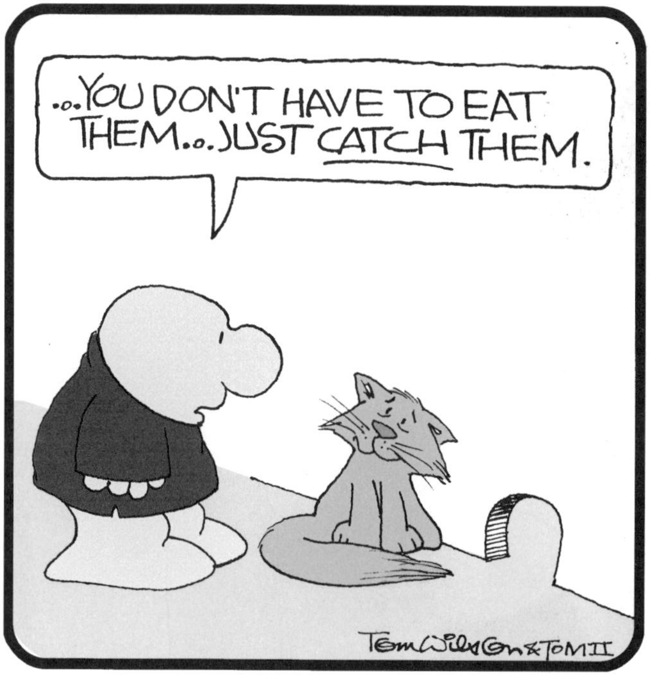
..o..YOU DON'T HAVE TO EAT THEM..o..JUST CATCH THEM.

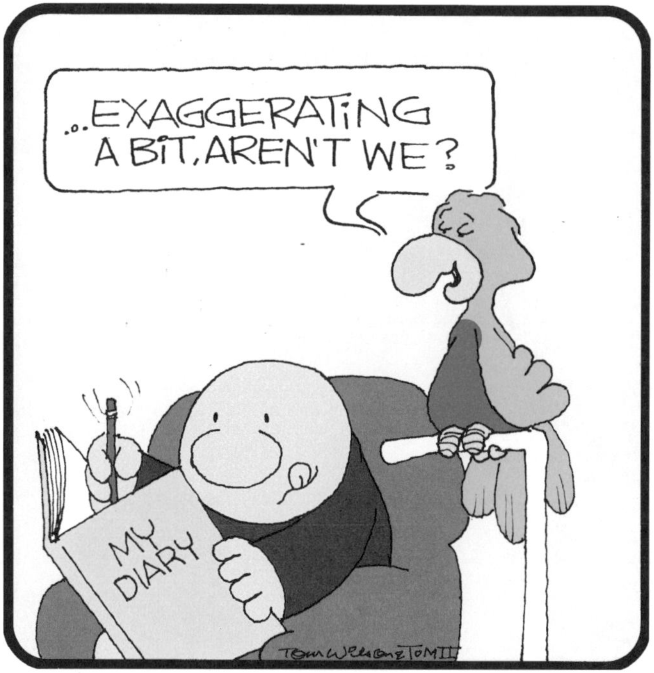
..o..EXAGGERATING A BIT, AREN'T WE?
MY DIARY

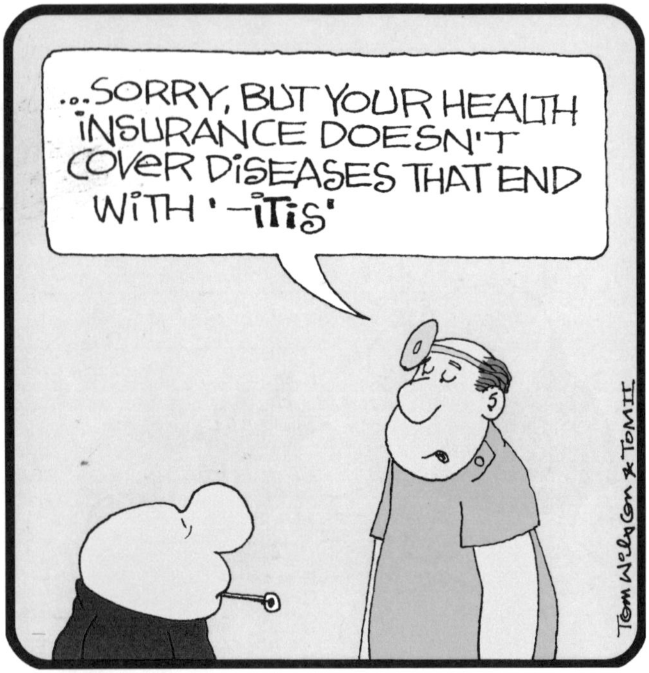
...SORRY, BUT YOUR HEALTH INSURANCE DOESN'T COVER DISEASES THAT END WITH '-ITIS'
TOM WILSON & TOM II

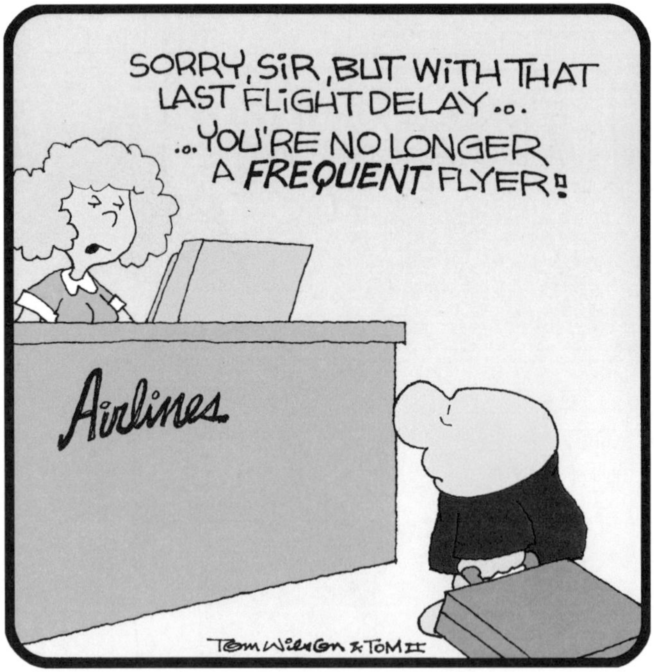
SORRY, SIR, BUT WITH THAT LAST FLIGHT DELAY...
...YOU'RE NO LONGER A FREQUENT FLYER!
Airlines
TOM WILSON & TOM II

EXCUSE ME, SIR!
..I COULDN'T HELP BUT NOTICE THAT DURING THE MOVIE, YOUR BIRD CRIED DURING ALL THE SAD PARTS...
..AND LAUGHED DURING THE FUNNY PARTS— HE SEEMED NOT ONLY TO UNDERSTAND THE MOVIE, BUT ENJOY IT.
..DON'T YOU FIND THAT A BIT UNUSUAL?
..I SURE DO!
..HE HATED THE BOOK!
Tom Wilson + Tom II

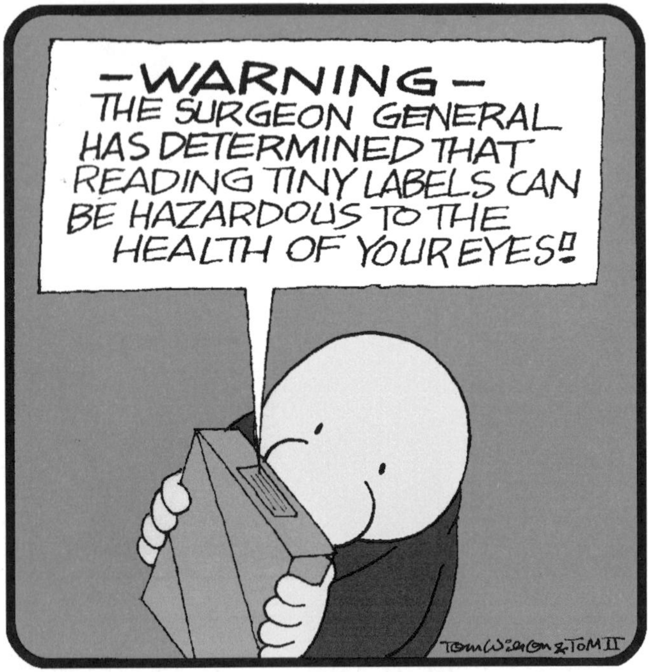
-WARNING-
THE SURGEON GENERAL HAS DETERMINED THAT READING TINY LABELS CAN BE HAZARDOUS TO THE HEALTH OF YOUR EYES!!
TOM WILSON & TOM II

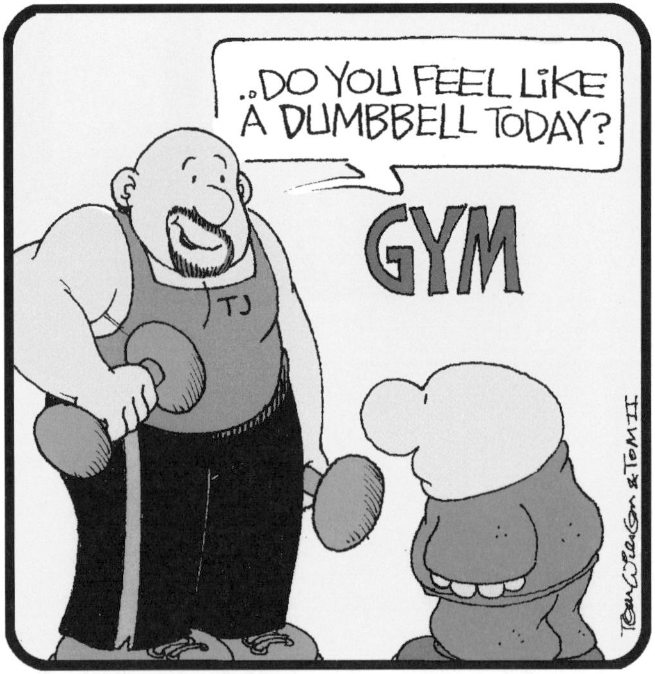
..DO YOU FEEL LIKE A DUMBBELL TODAY?
GYM
TJ
TOM WILSON & TOM II

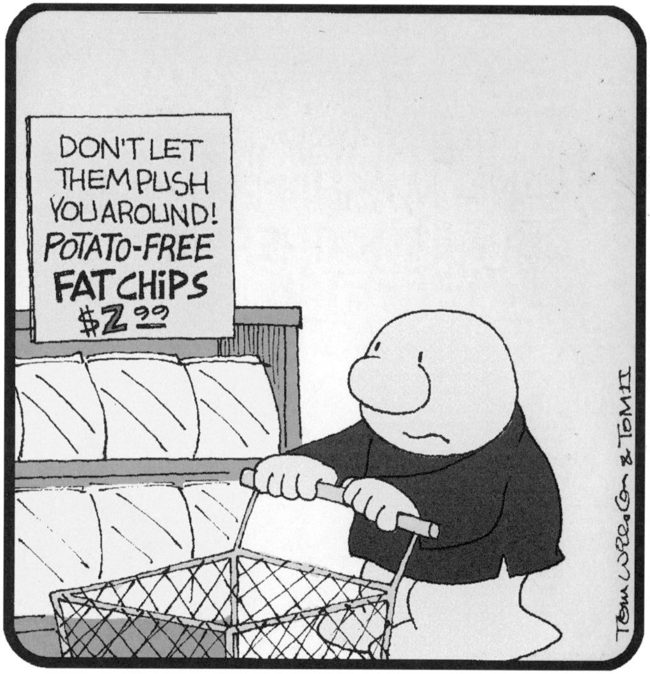
DON'T LET THEM PUSH YOU AROUND! POTATO-FREE FAT CHIPS $2.99
TOM WILSON & TOM II

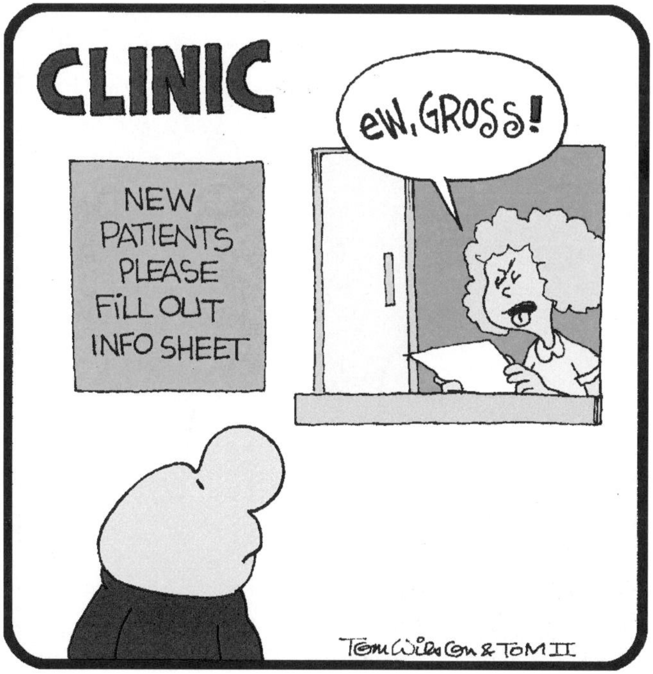
CLINIC
EW, GROSS!
NEW PATIENTS PLEASE FILL OUT INFO SHEET
TOM WILSON & TOM II

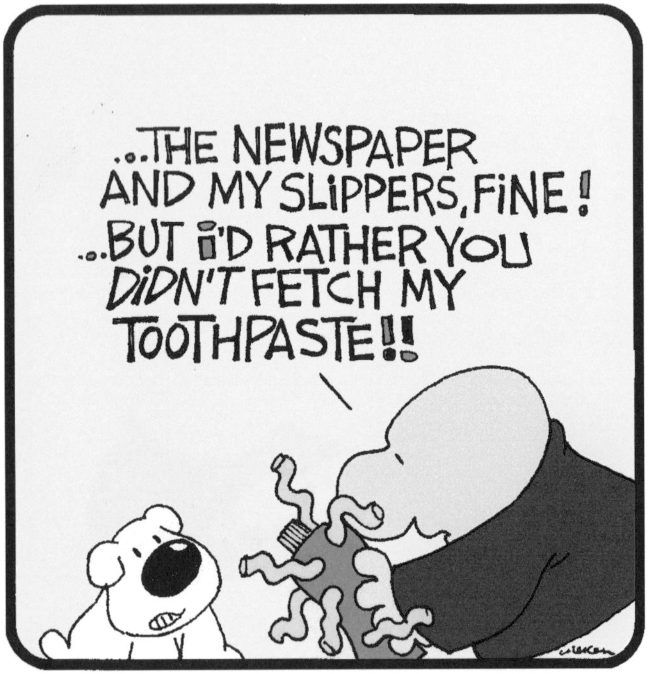
..THE NEWSPAPER AND MY SLIPPERS, FINE! ..BUT I'D RATHER YOU DIDN'T FETCH MY TOOTHPASTE!!

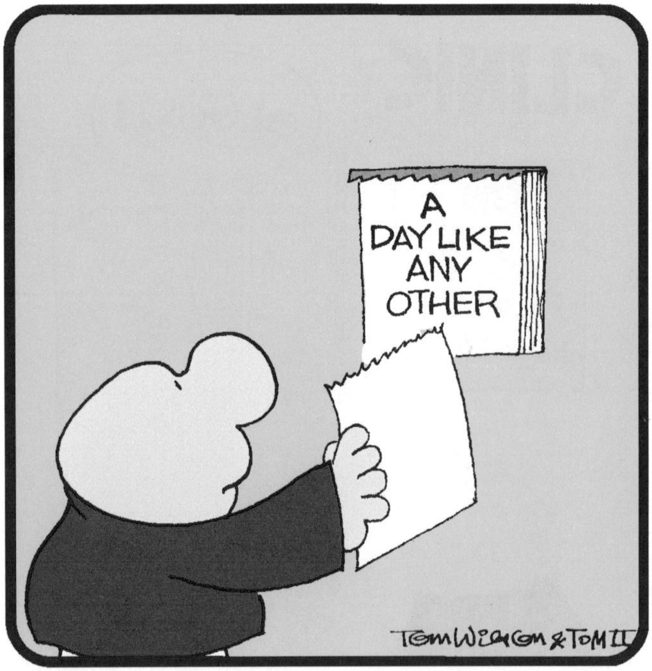
A DAY LIKE ANY OTHER
TOM WILSON & TOM II

..AS WE TRAVEL THROUGH LIFE..

..WHAT WE BEGIN THE JOURNEY WITH..

..WHAT WE TAKE WITH US..

...AND WHAT WE PICK UP ALONG THE WAY..

..IS NEVER MORE IMPORTANT THAN WHAT WE LEAVE BEHIND!!

CAT NIP   SID   FUZZ

"AS WE'VE TRAVELED ALONG LIFE'S PATH, HOW GRATEFUL I AM FOR YOUR COMPANY AND HOW GRATEFUL I AM FOR YOUR BRINGING ALONG WHAT I LACK. ...BUT MOST OF ALL, I'M GRATEFUL FOR WHAT YOU'VE LEFT BEHIND WHEN WE HAD TO PART... FOR THOSE PROVISIONS SUSTAIN ME ON MY JOURNEY AND LIGHTEN MY BURDEN. FOR SUSAN AND ALL MY BEAUTIFUL FELLOW TRAVELERS IN LIFE. ~T.W.

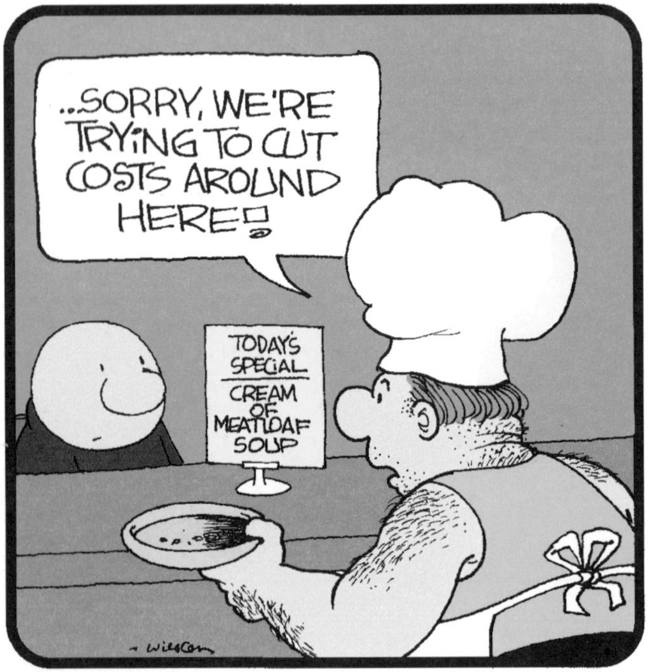
..SORRY, WE'RE TRYING TO CUT COSTS AROUND HERE!
TODAY'S SPECIAL
CREAM OF MEATLOAF SOUP

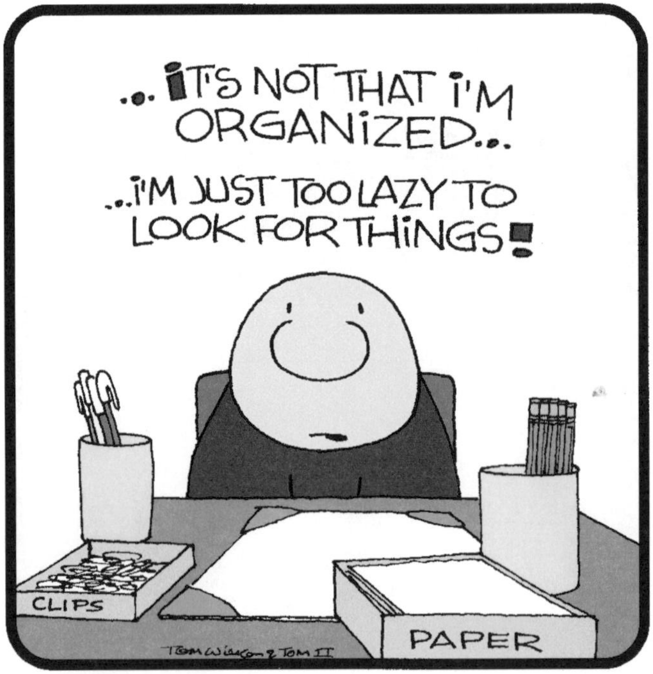
..IT'S NOT THAT I'M ORGANIZED...
..I'M JUST TOO LAZY TO LOOK FOR THINGS!
CLIPS
PAPER
TOM WILSON & TOM II

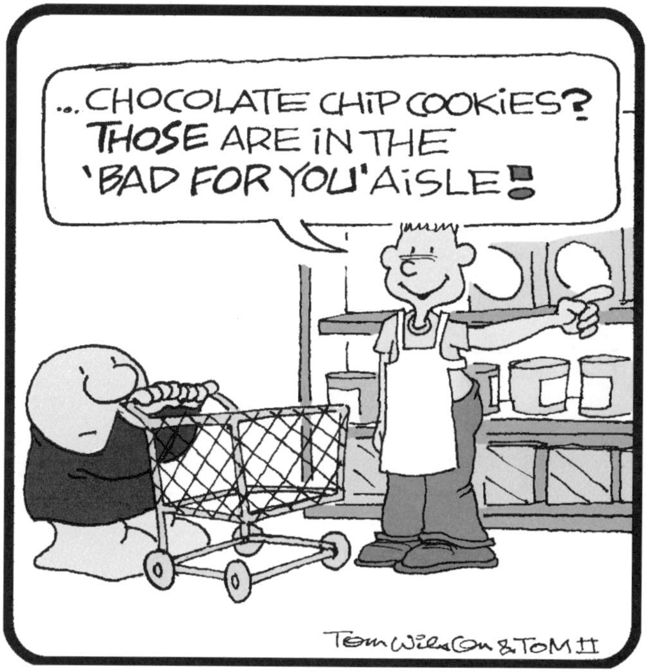
...CHOCOLATE CHIP COOKIES? THOSE ARE IN THE 'BAD FOR YOU' AISLE!
TOM WILSON & TOM II

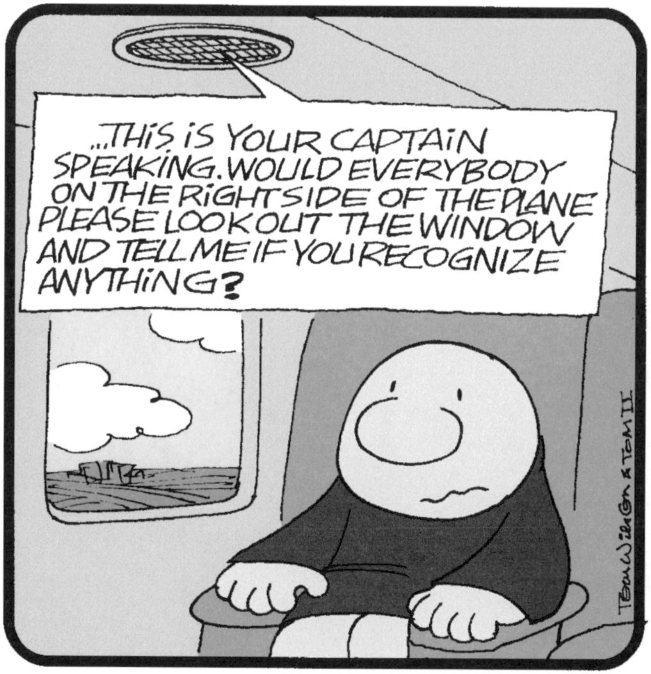
...THIS IS YOUR CAPTAIN SPEAKING. WOULD EVERYBODY ON THE RIGHT SIDE OF THE PLANE PLEASE LOOK OUT THE WINDOW AND TELL ME IF YOU RECOGNIZE ANYTHING?
TOM WILSON & TOM II

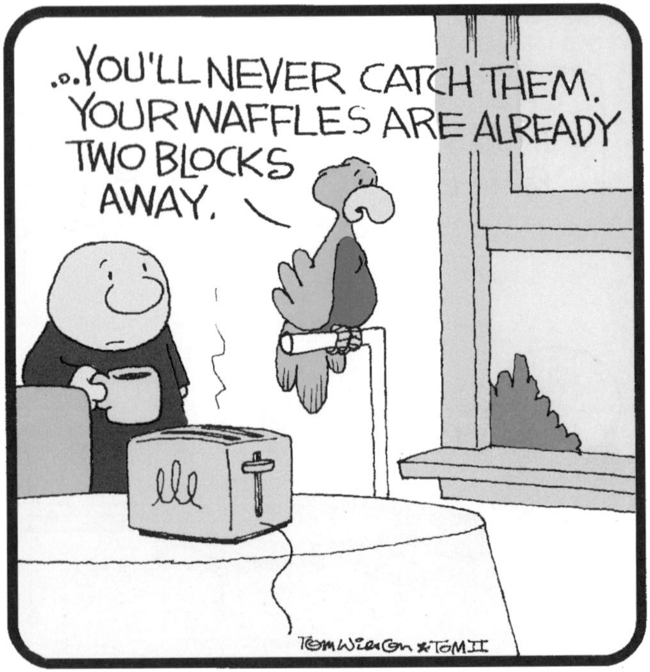
...YOU'LL NEVER CATCH THEM. YOUR WAFFLES ARE ALREADY TWO BLOCKS AWAY.
TOM WILSON & TOM II

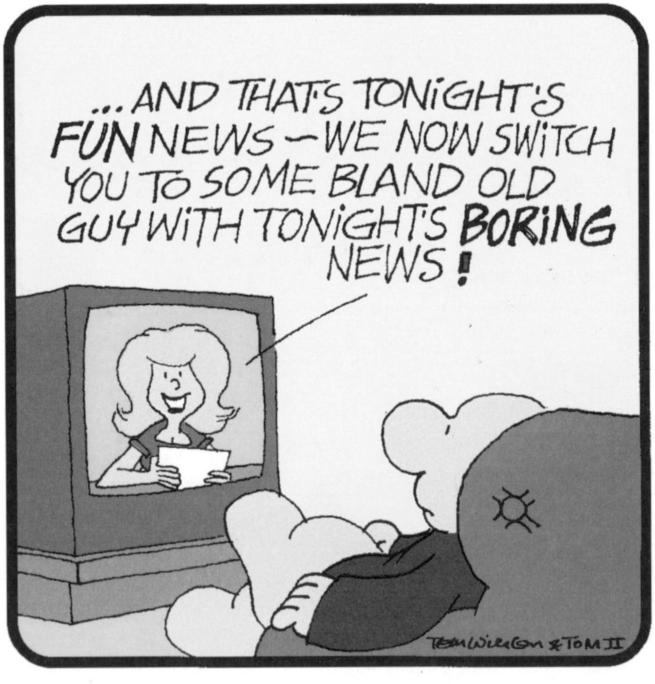
...AND THAT'S TONIGHT'S FUN NEWS—WE NOW SWITCH YOU TO SOME BLAND OLD GUY WITH TONIGHT'S BORING NEWS!
TOM WILSON & TOM II

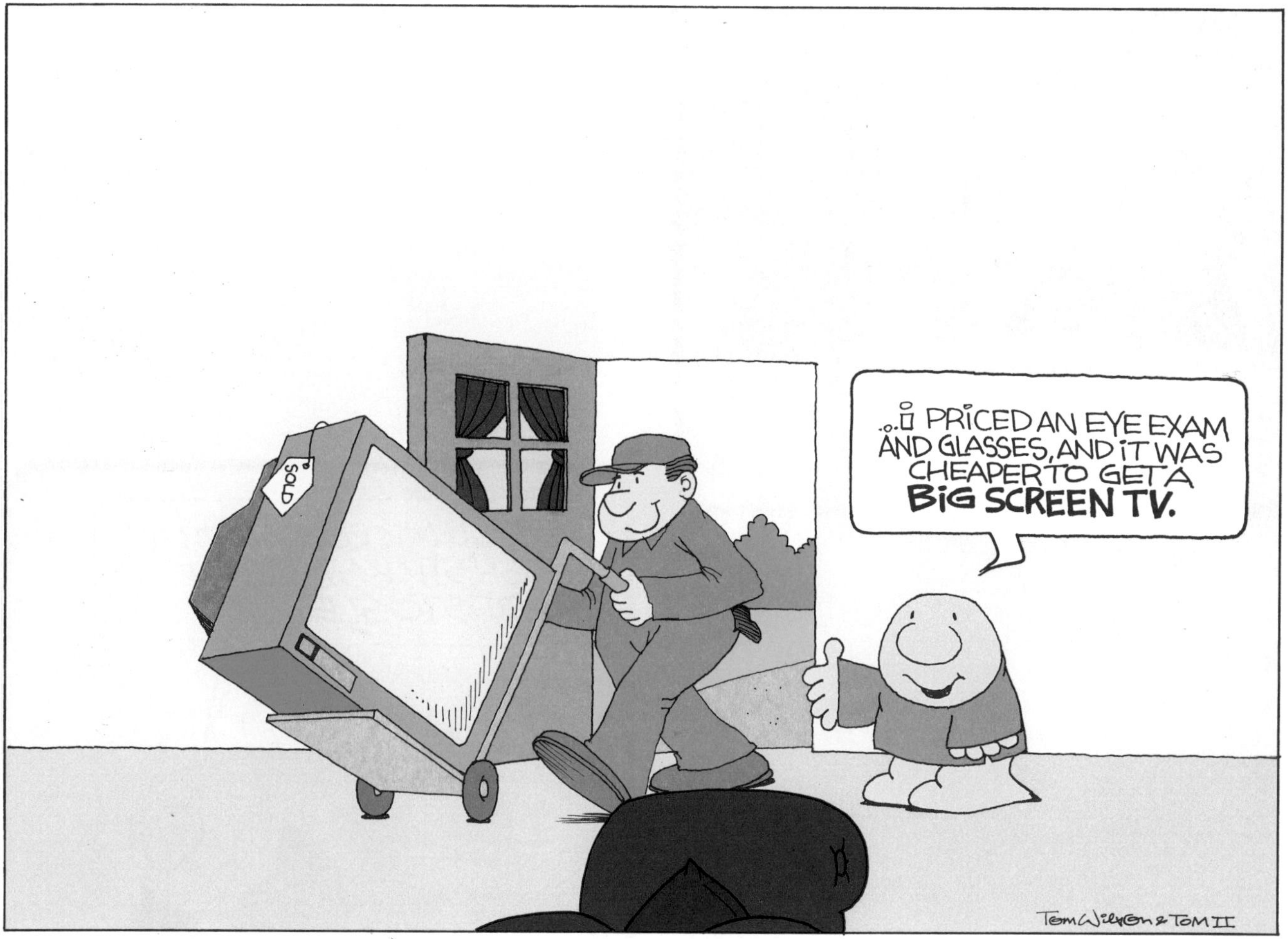

SOLD
..I PRICED AN EYE EXAM AND GLASSES, AND IT WAS CHEAPER TO GET A **BIG SCREEN TV.**

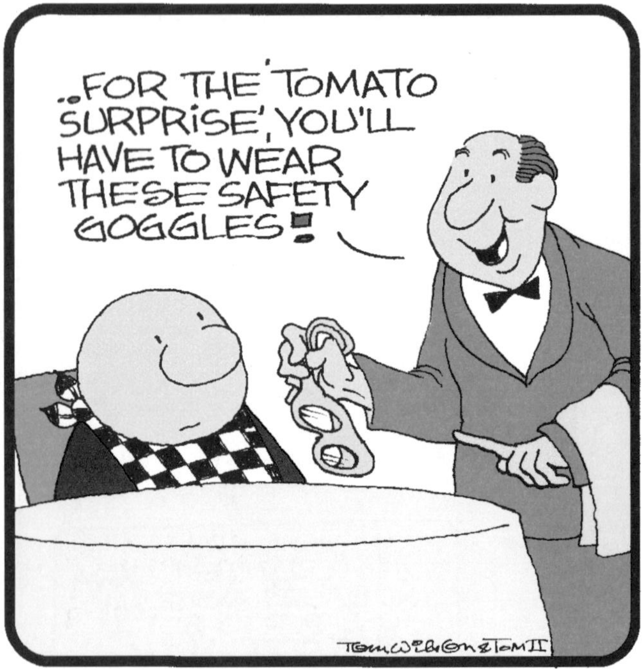
..FOR THE 'TOMATO SURPRISE', YOU'LL HAVE TO WEAR THESE SAFETY GOGGLES!!
TOM WILSON & TOM II

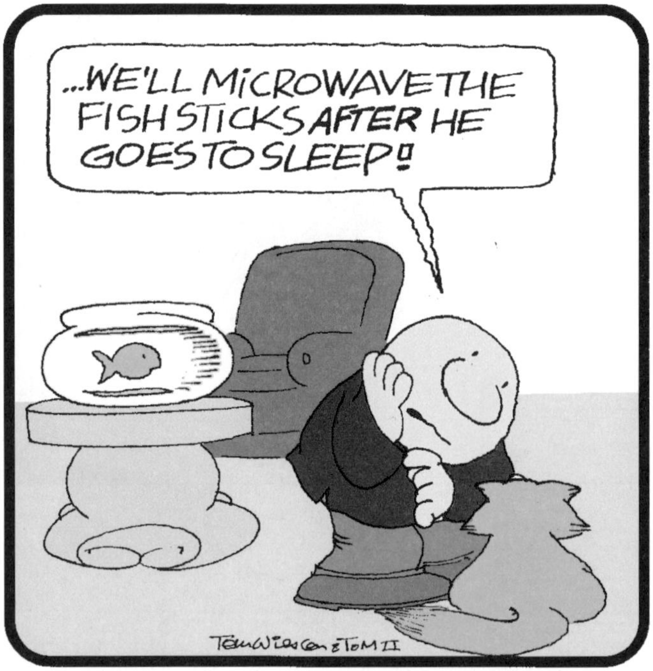
...WE'LL MICROWAVE THE FISH STICKS **AFTER** HE GOES TO SLEEP!!
TOM WILSON & TOM II

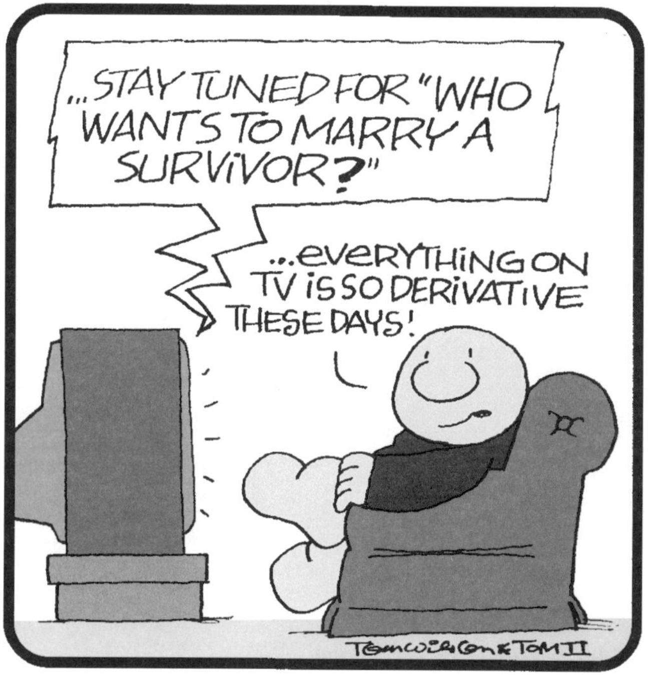
...STAY TUNED FOR "WHO WANTS TO MARRY A SURVIVOR?"
...everything on TV is so derivative these days!
Tom Wilson & Tom II

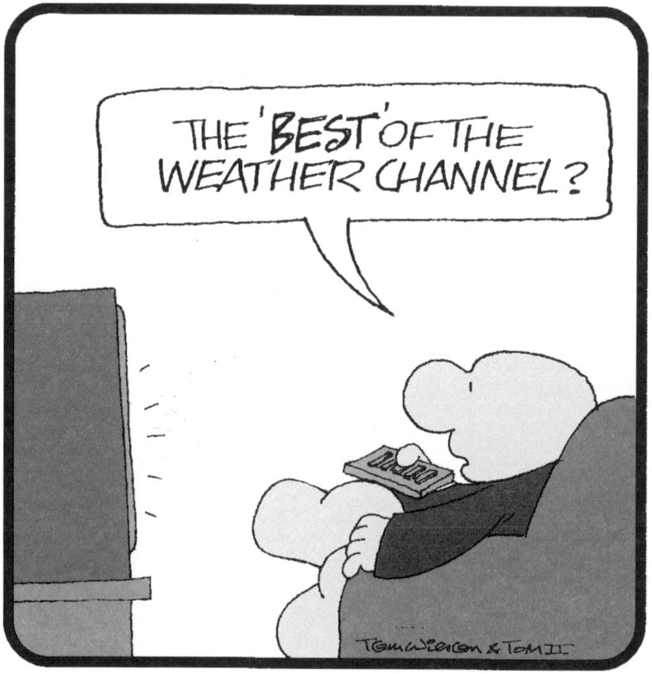
THE 'BEST' OF THE WEATHER CHANNEL?
Tom Wilson & Tom II

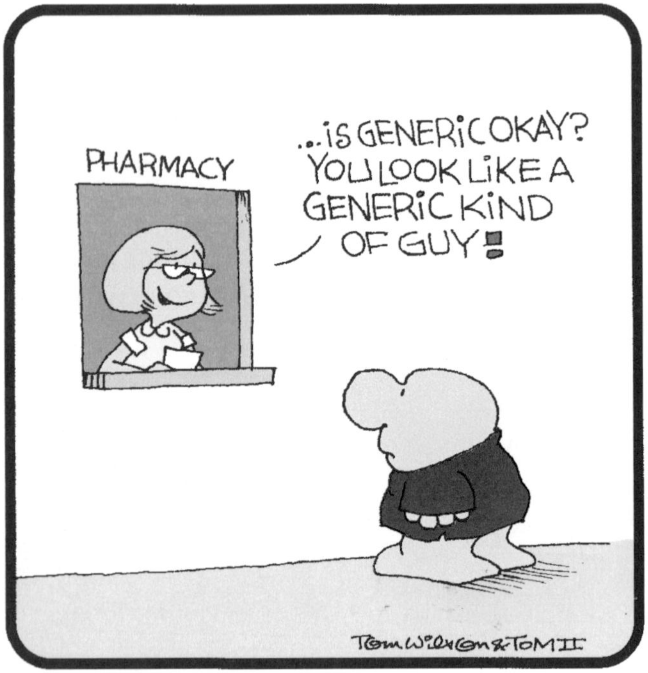
PHARMACY
...IS GENERIC OKAY? YOU LOOK LIKE A GENERIC KIND OF GUY!
TOM WILSON & TOM II

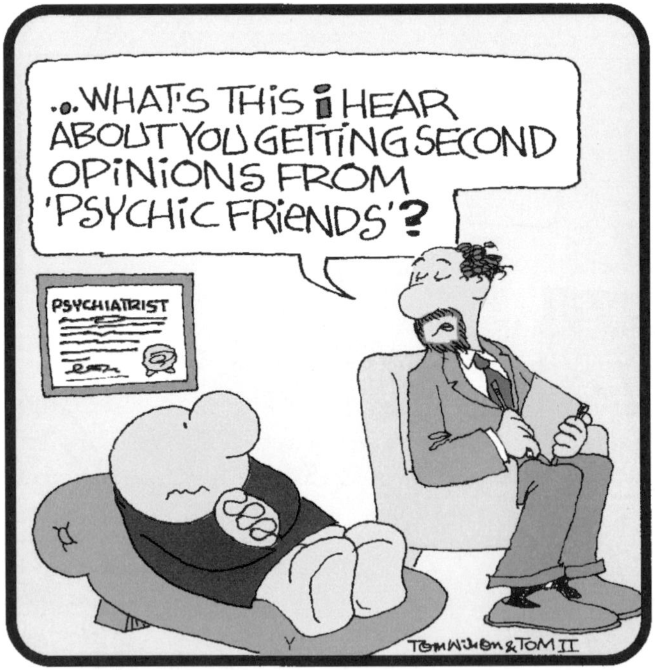
...WHAT'S THIS I HEAR ABOUT YOU GETTING SECOND OPINIONS FROM 'PSYCHIC FRIENDS'?
PSYCHIATRIST
TOM WILSON & TOM II

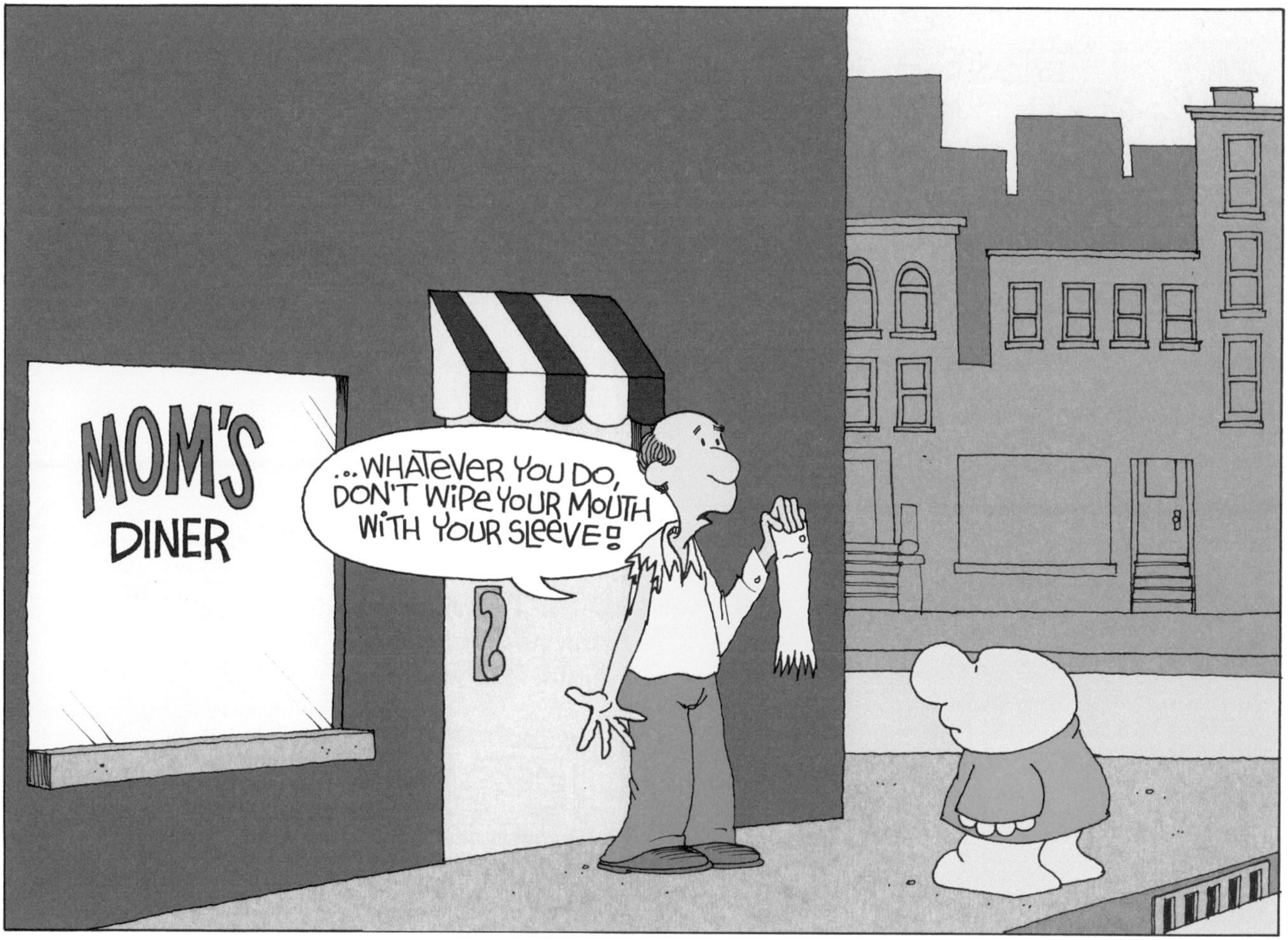
MOM'S
DINER
...WHATEVER YOU DO, DON'T WIPE YOUR MOUTH WITH YOUR SLEEVE!!

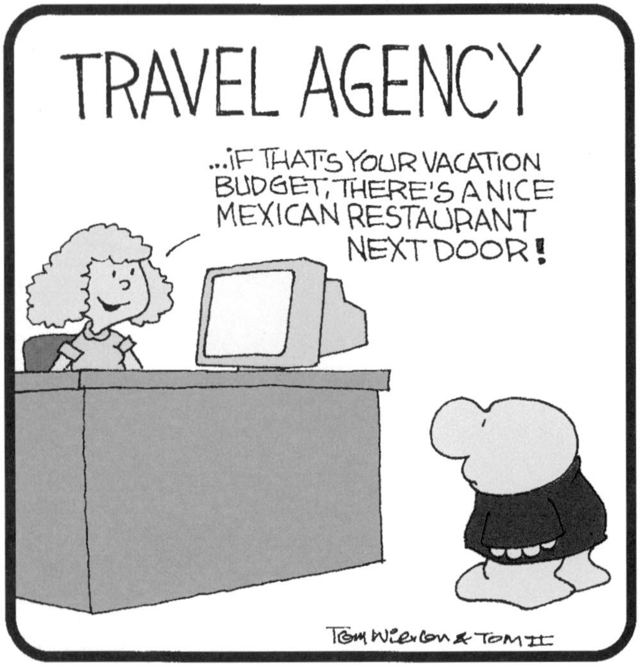
TRAVEL AGENCY
...IF THAT'S YOUR VACATION BUDGET, THERE'S A NICE MEXICAN RESTAURANT NEXT DOOR!
Tom Wilson & Tom II

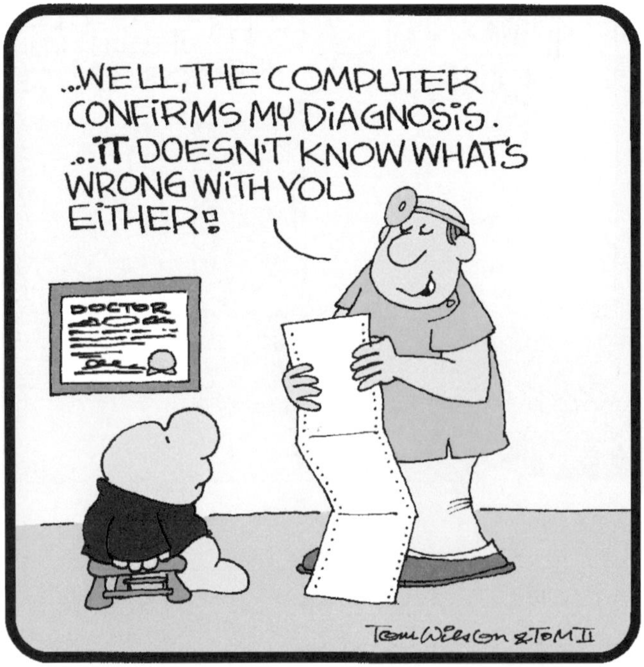
..WELL, THE COMPUTER CONFIRMS MY DIAGNOSIS. ...IT DOESN'T KNOW WHAT'S WRONG WITH YOU EITHER!
DOCTOR
Tom Wilson & Tom II

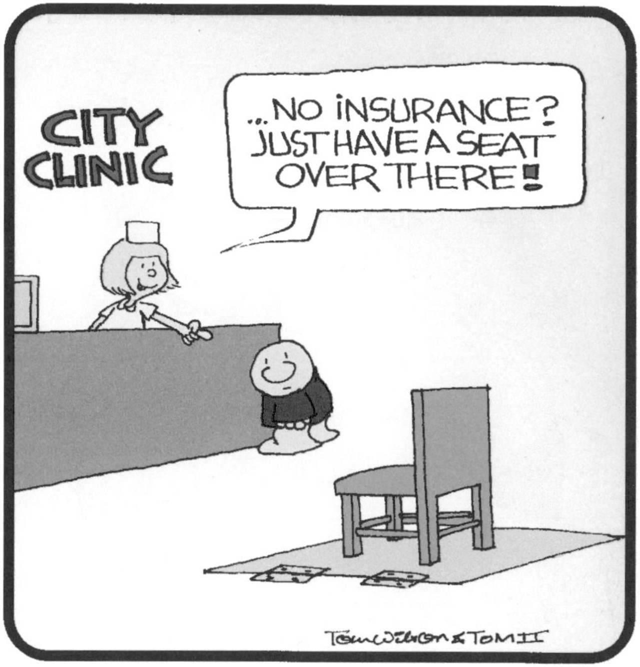
CITY CLINIC
...NO INSURANCE? JUST HAVE A SEAT OVER THERE!
TOM WILSON & TOM II

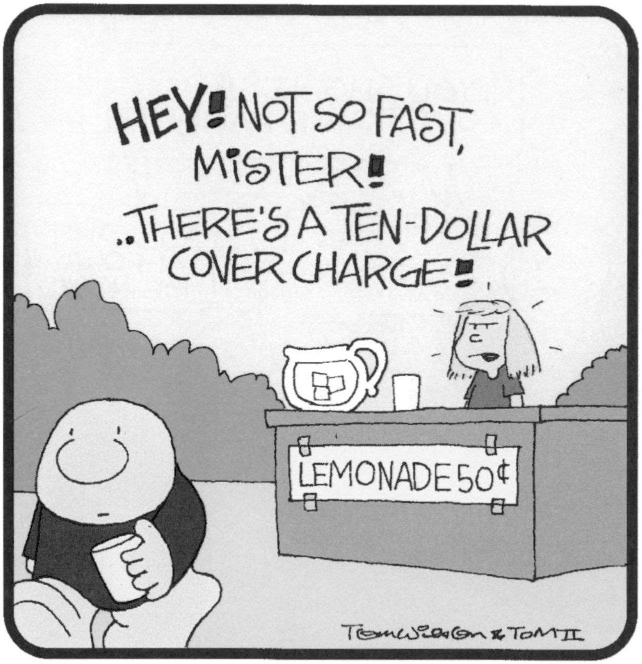
HEY! NOT SO FAST, MISTER! ..THERE'S A TEN-DOLLAR COVER CHARGE!
LEMONADE 50¢
TOM WILSON & TOM II

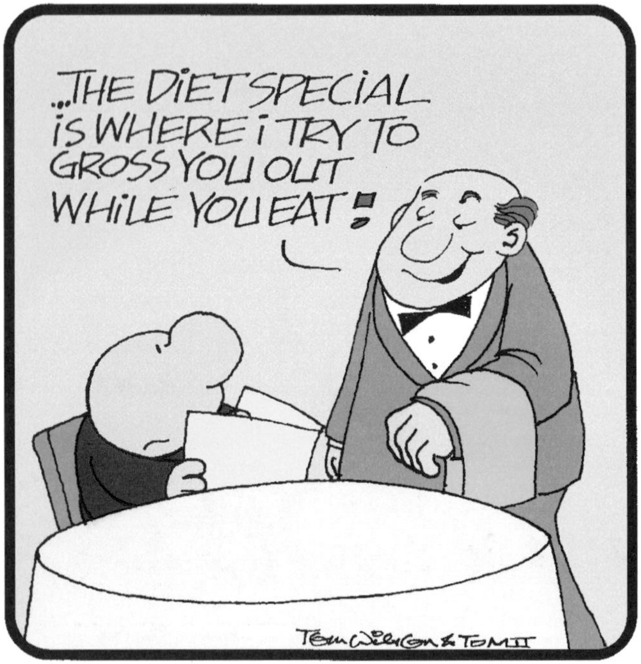
...THE DIET SPECIAL iS WHERE i TRY TO GROSS YOU OUT WHiLE YOU EAT!
TOM WILSON & TOM II

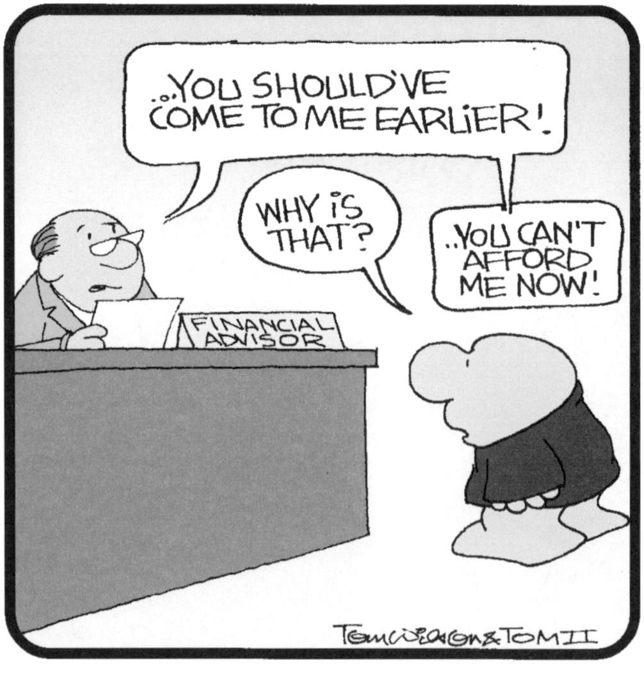
...YOU SHOULD'VE COME TO ME EARLiER!
WHY iS THAT?
..YOU CAN'T AFFORD ME NOW!
FINANCIAL ADVISOR
TOM WILSON & TOM II

CHRISTMAS IS A SPECIAL TIME OF YEAR!
..FOR SOME, IT'S ALL ABOUT THE **PRESENT**!
..FOR OTHERS, CHRISTMAS IS A TIME TO DREAM OF THE **FUTURE**!
DEC 24
BUT CHRISTMAS IS ALSO A TIME TO THINK BACK & REMEMBER...
LIL' ZIG
ALL THE PEOPLE AND MEMORIES FROM ALL OUR CHRISTMASES **PAST**!
...ABOVE ALL, CHRISTMAS IS MUCH MORE THAN A **SPECIAL TIME** OF **YEAR**...
..IT'S **YEARS** OF **SPECIAL TIMES**!

BARBER
...IT'S BEEN A SLOW DAY, PAL—HOW ABOUT A NICE POLISH?
TOM WILSON & TOM II

CANDY
75¢
ASK ABOUT OUR EASY PAYMENT PLAN
TOM WILSON & TOM II

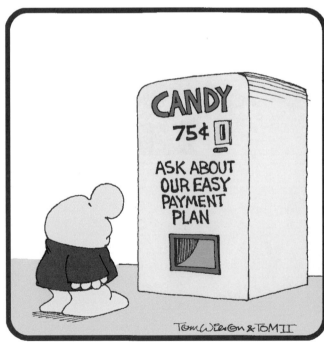

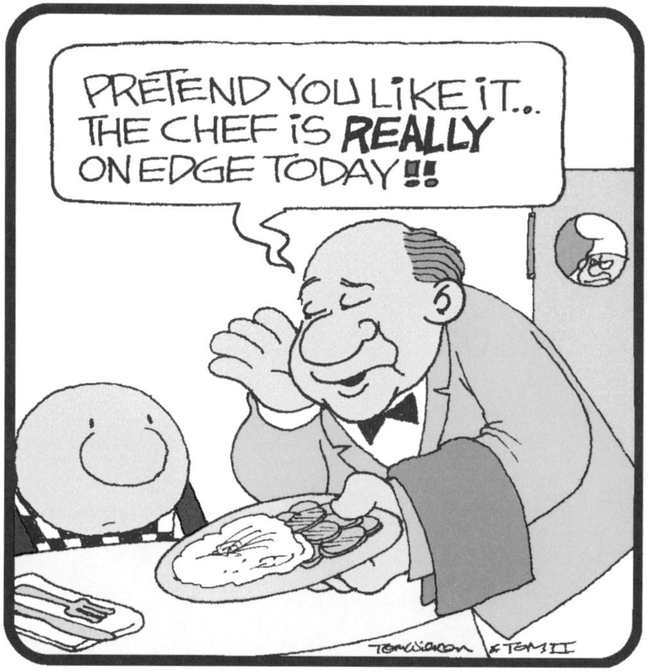
PRETEND YOU LIKE IT... THE CHEF IS **REALLY** ON EDGE TODAY!!
TOM WILSON & TOM II

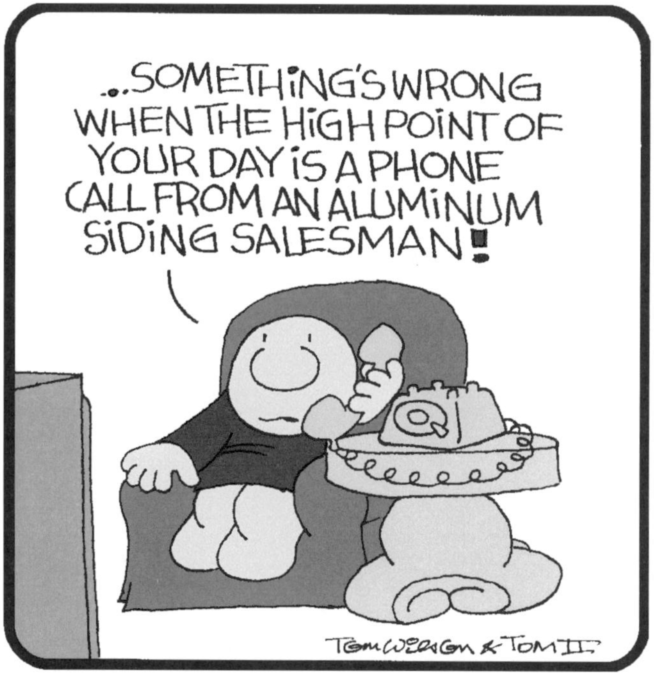
...SOMETHING'S WRONG WHEN THE HIGH POINT OF YOUR DAY IS A PHONE CALL FROM AN ALUMINUM SIDING SALESMAN!
TOM WILSON & TOM II

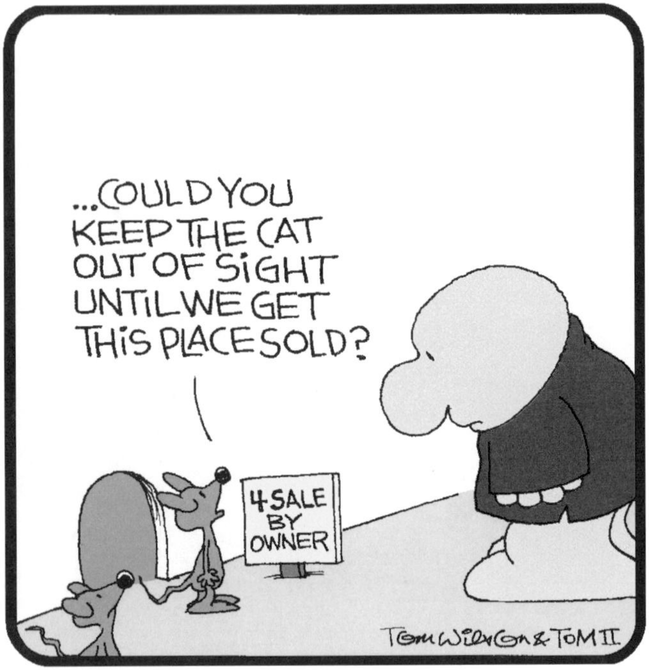
...COULD YOU KEEP THE CAT OUT OF SIGHT UNTIL WE GET THIS PLACE SOLD?
4 SALE BY OWNER
TOM WILSON & TOM II

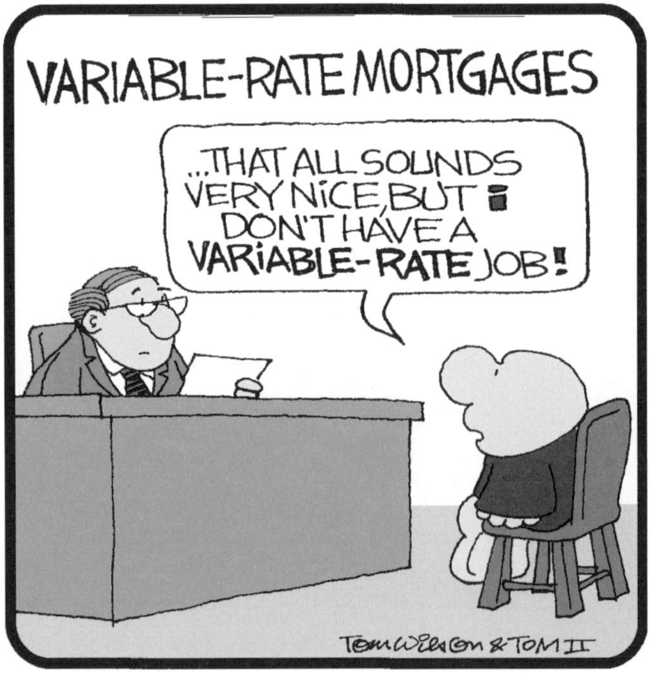
VARIABLE-RATE MORTGAGES
...THAT ALL SOUNDS VERY NICE, BUT I DON'T HAVE A VARIABLE-RATE JOB!
TOM WILSON & TOM II

..WELCOME, MY SON... HOW ARE YOU TODAY?
TERRIBLE! MY BOSS JUST CUT MY PAY AND GAVE HIMSELF A RAISE.
..THEN HE DEMOTED ME AND GAVE HIS NEPHEW MY JOB AND MADE HIM MY BOSS.
I NEED SOME WORDS OF WISDOM.
CHEER UP, MY SON! "TIME HEALS ALL WOUNDS."
...I GUESS THAT HELPS, BUT I'M STILL MAD AT MY BOSS... HE SEEMS TO GET AWAY WITH EVERYTHING!
I GOTCHA COVERED...
"TIME WOUNDS ALL HEELS"!

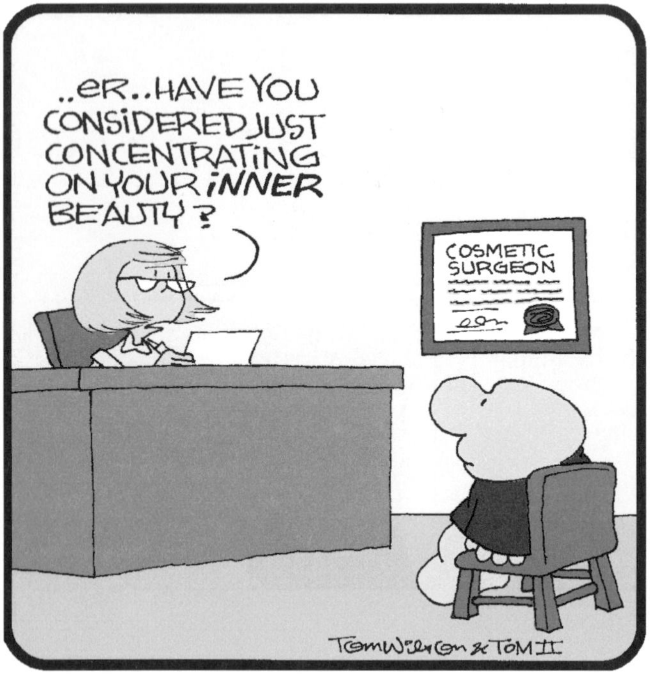
..er..HAVE YOU CONSIDERED JUST CONCENTRATING ON YOUR iNNER BEAUTY ?
COSMETIC SURGEON
TOM WILSON & TOM II

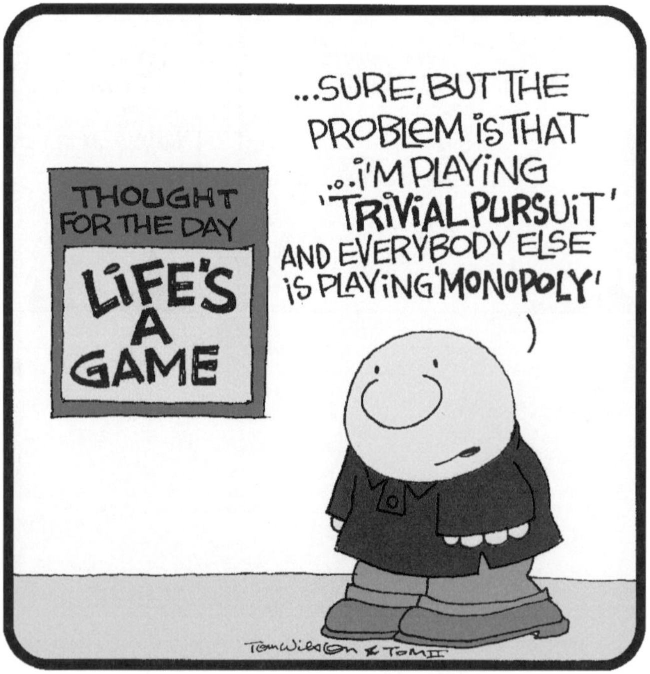
THOUGHT FOR THE DAY
LIFE'S A GAME
...SURE, BUT THE PROBLEM IS THAT ..i'M PLAYING 'TRIVIAL PURSUIT' AND EVERYBODY ELSE IS PLAYING 'MONOPOLY'
TOM WILSON & TOM II

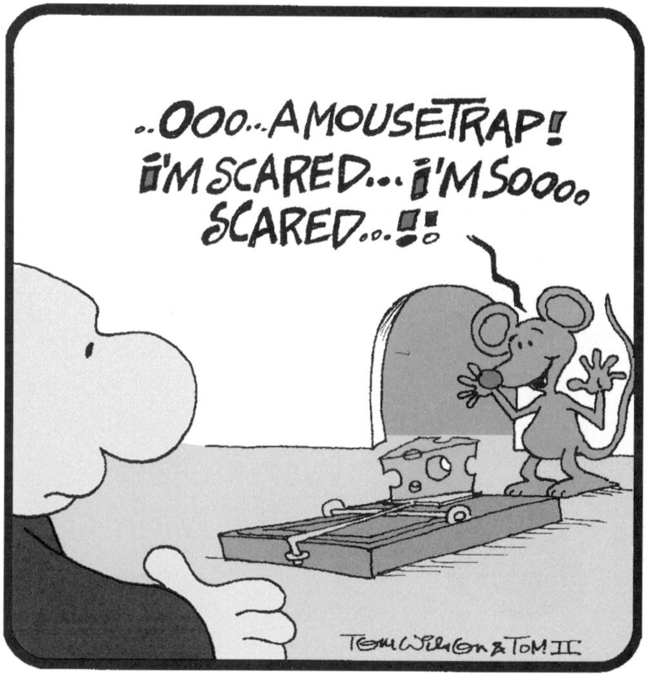
..OOO...A MOUSETRAP!
I'M SCARED... I'M SOOOO
SCARED...!!
TOM WILSON & TOM II

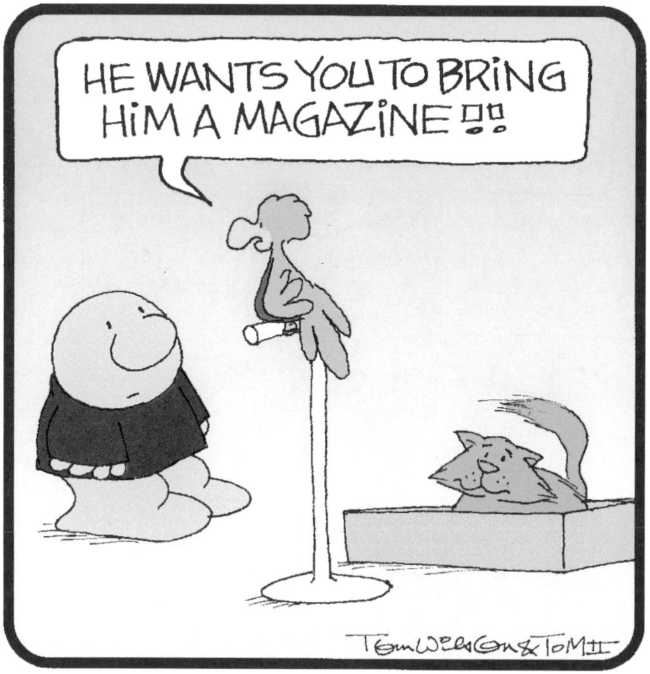
HE WANTS YOU TO BRING HIM A MAGAZINE!!
TOM WILSON & TOM II

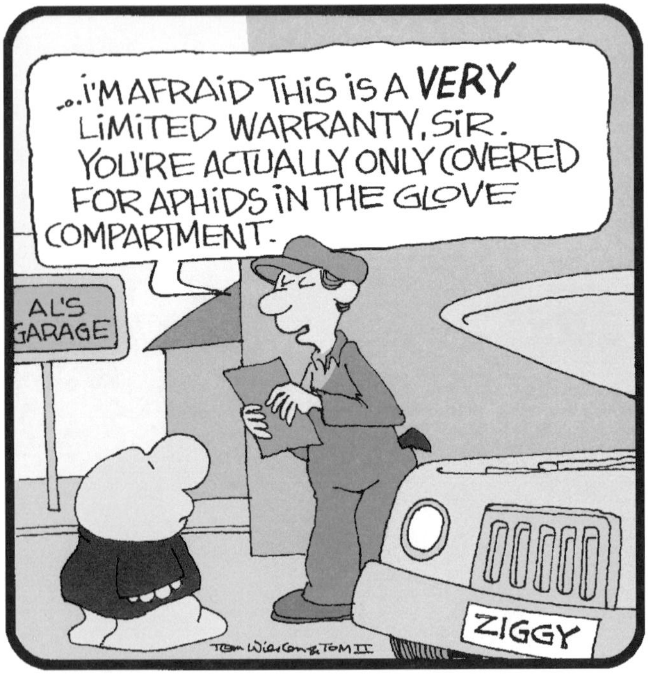
...I'M AFRAID THIS IS A VERY LIMITED WARRANTY, SIR. YOU'RE ACTUALLY ONLY COVERED FOR APHIDS IN THE GLOVE COMPARTMENT.
AL'S GARAGE
ZIGGY
TOM WILSON & TOM II

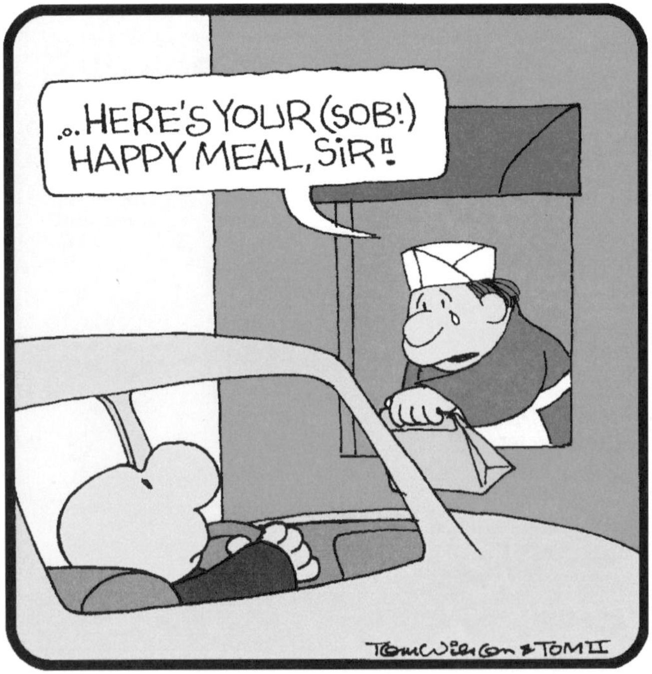
...HERE'S YOUR (SOB!) HAPPY MEAL, SIR!!
TOM WILSON & TOM II

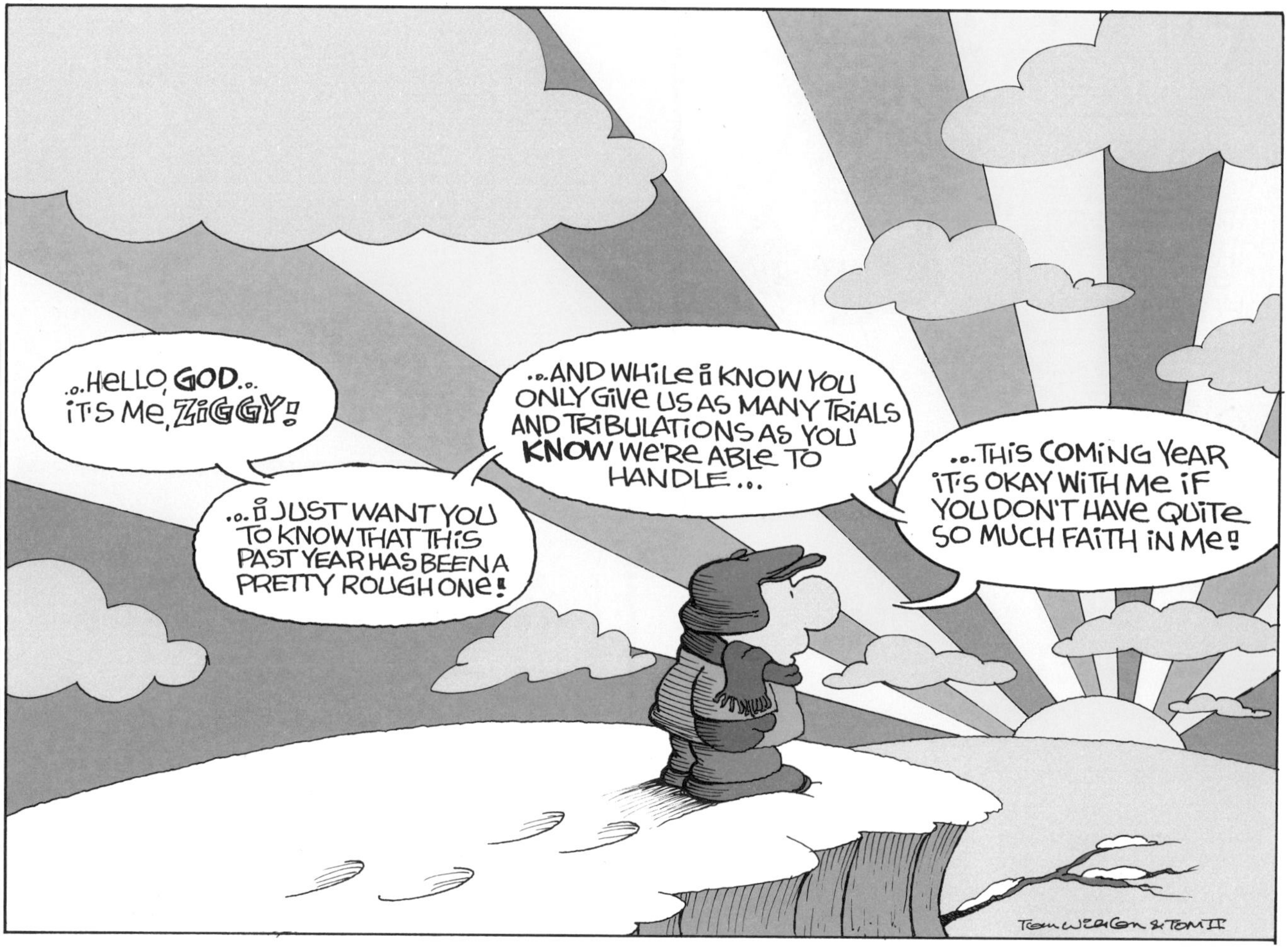
...HELLO, GOD... IT'S ME, ZIGGY!
...I JUST WANT YOU TO KNOW THAT THIS PAST YEAR HAS BEEN A PRETTY ROUGH ONE!
...AND WHILE I KNOW YOU ONLY GIVE US AS MANY TRIALS AND TRIBULATIONS AS YOU KNOW WE'RE ABLE TO HANDLE...
...THIS COMING YEAR IT'S OKAY WITH ME IF YOU DON'T HAVE QUITE SO MUCH FAITH IN ME!

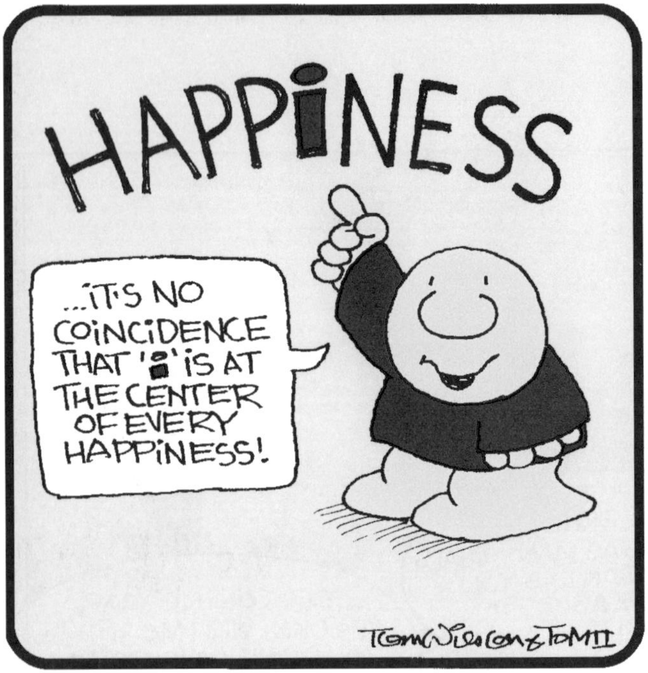
HAPPiNESS
...iT'S NO COiNCiDENCE THAT 'i' iS AT THE CENTER OF EVERY HAPPiNESS!
TOM WILSON & TOM II

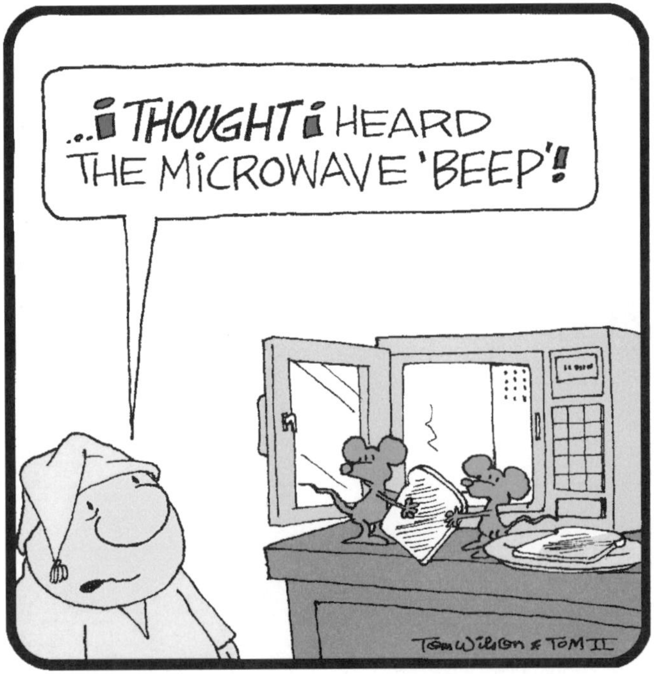
...i THOUGHT i HEARD THE MiCROWAVE 'BEEP'!
TOM WILSON & TOM II

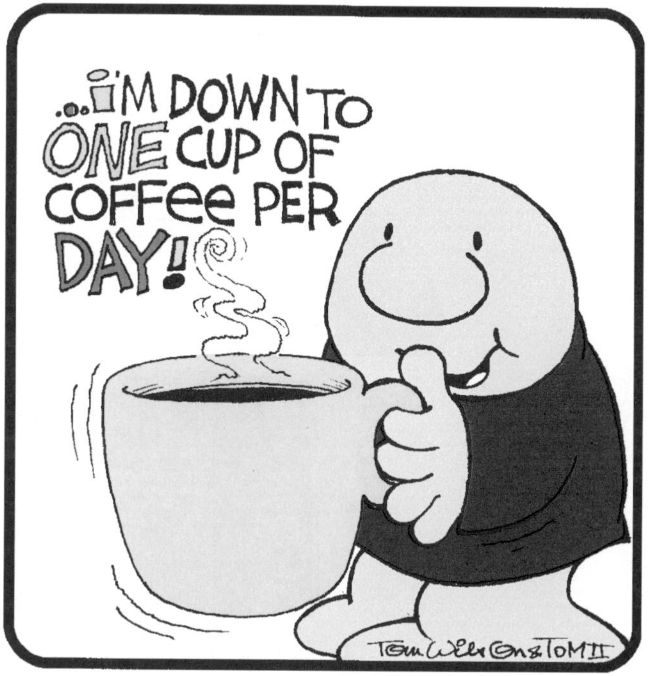
...I'M DOWN TO ONE CUP OF COFFEE PER DAY!
TOM WILSON & TOM II

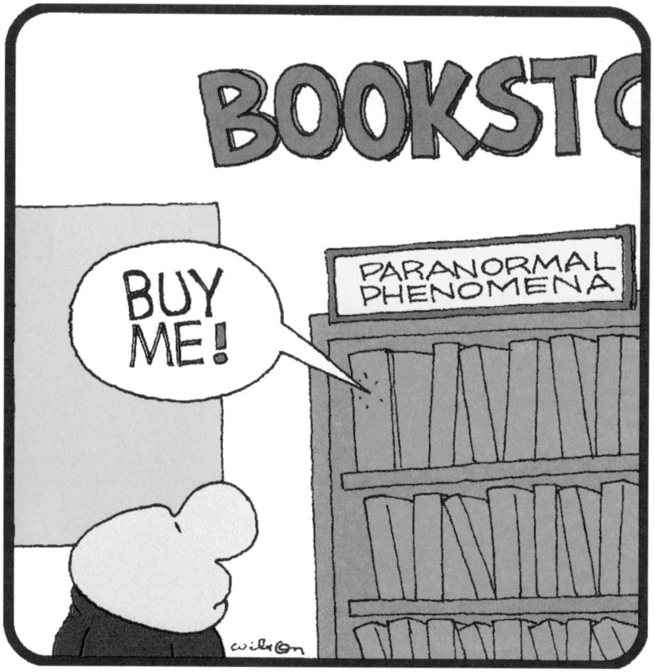
BOOKSTO
PARANORMAL PHENOMENA
BUY ME!
wilson

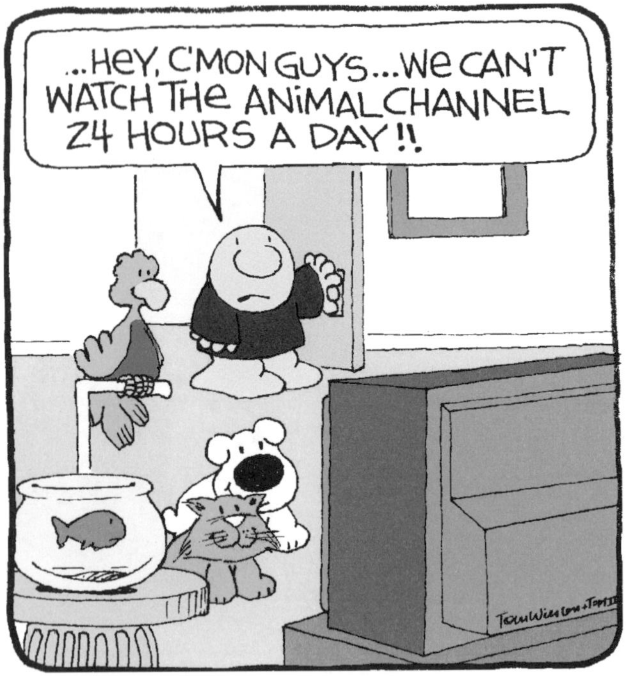
...HEY, C'MON GUYS...WE CAN'T WATCH THE ANIMAL CHANNEL 24 HOURS A DAY!!

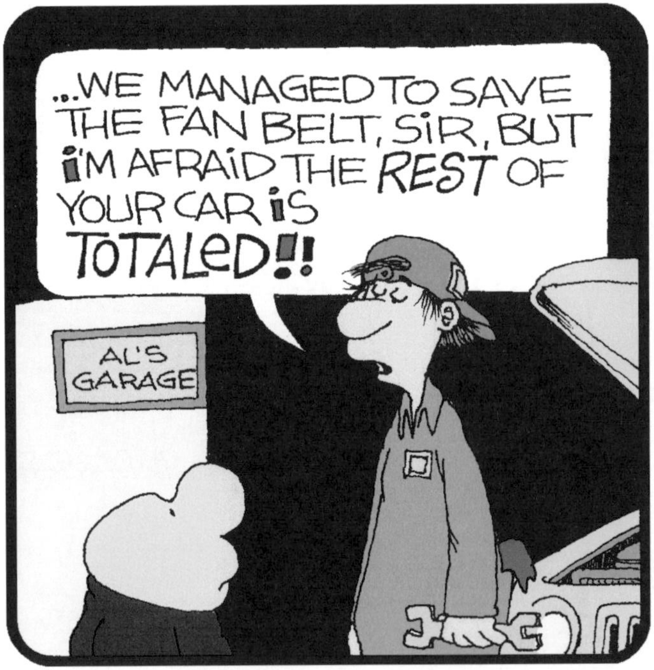
...WE MANAGED TO SAVE THE FAN BELT, SIR, BUT I'M AFRAID THE *REST* OF YOUR CAR IS TOTALED!!!
AL'S GARAGE

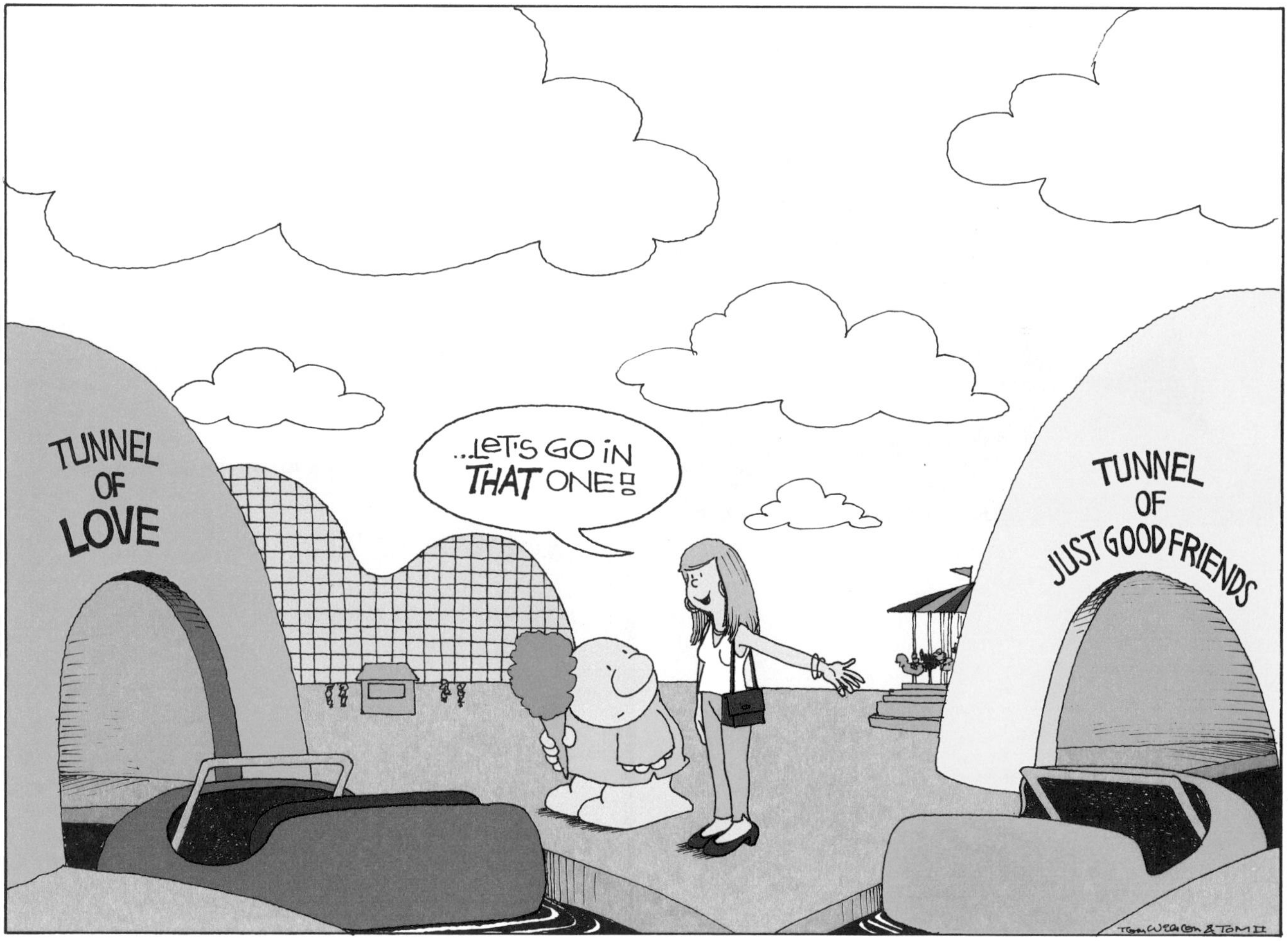
TUNNEL OF LOVE
...LET'S GO IN THAT ONE!!
TUNNEL OF JUST GOOD FRIENDS

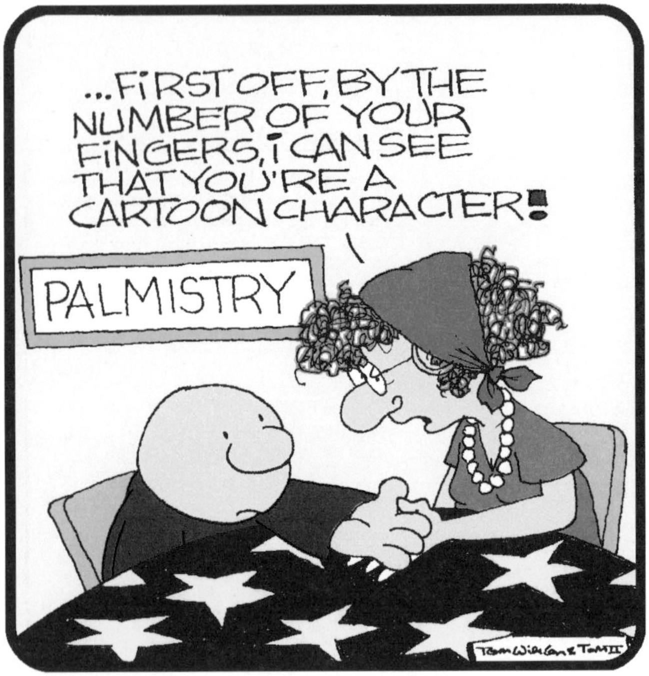
...FIRST OFF, BY THE NUMBER OF YOUR FINGERS, I CAN SEE THAT YOU'RE A CARTOON CHARACTER!
PALMISTRY

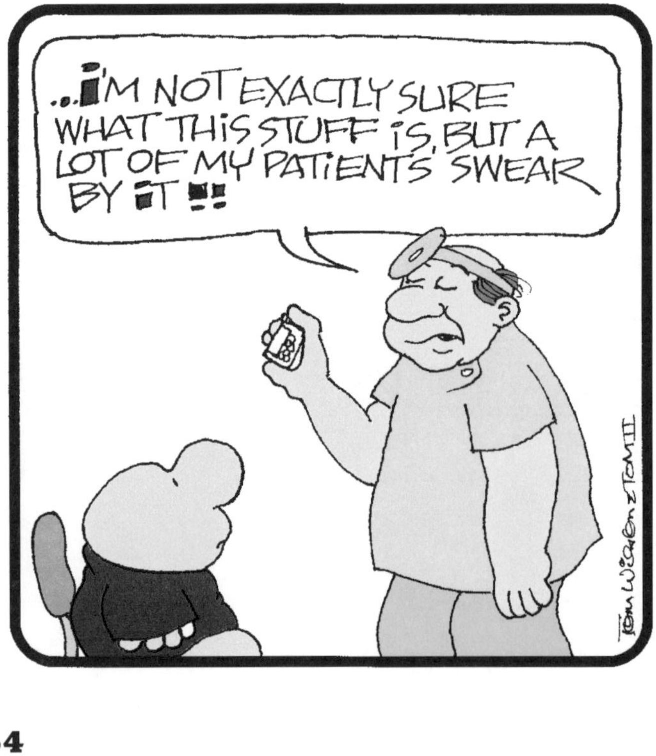
..I'M NOT EXACTLY SURE WHAT THIS STUFF IS, BUT A LOT OF MY PATIENTS SWEAR BY IT!!

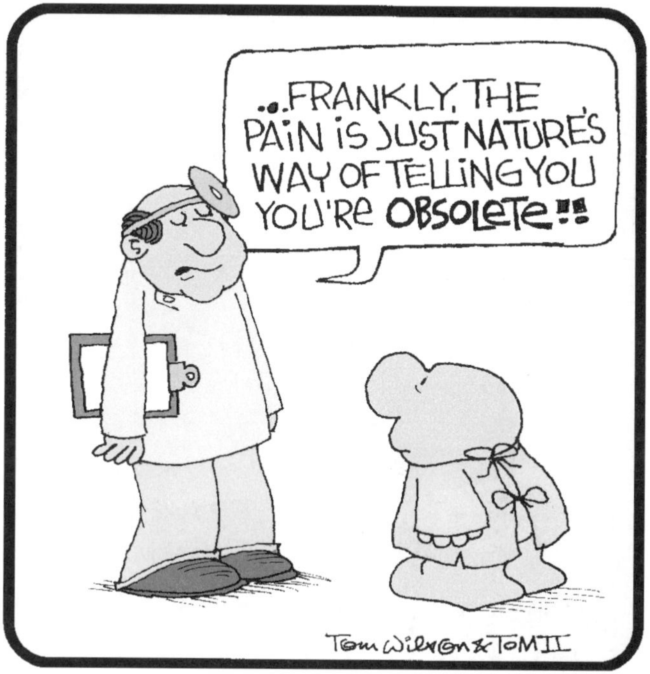
..FRANKLY, THE PAIN IS JUST NATURE'S WAY OF TELLING YOU YOU'RE **OBSOLETE!!**
Tom Wilson & Tom II

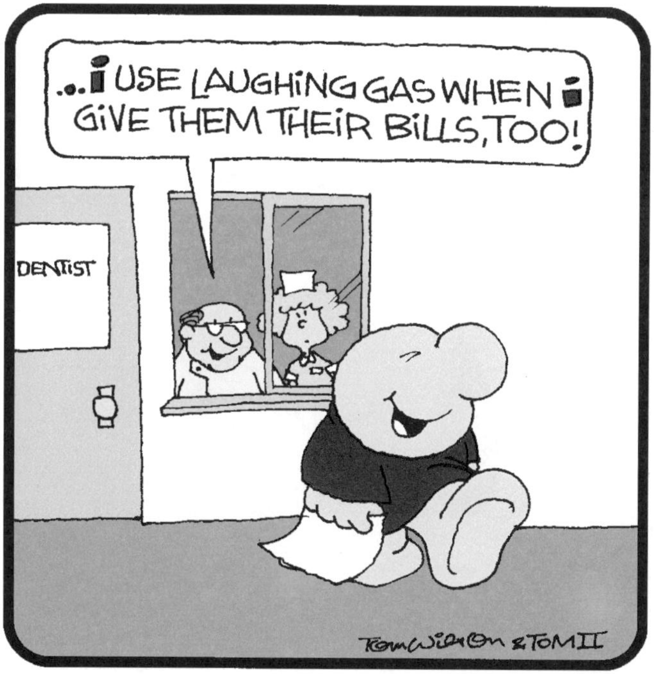
..I USE LAUGHING GAS WHEN I GIVE THEM THEIR BILLS, TOO!
DENTIST
Tom Wilson & Tom II

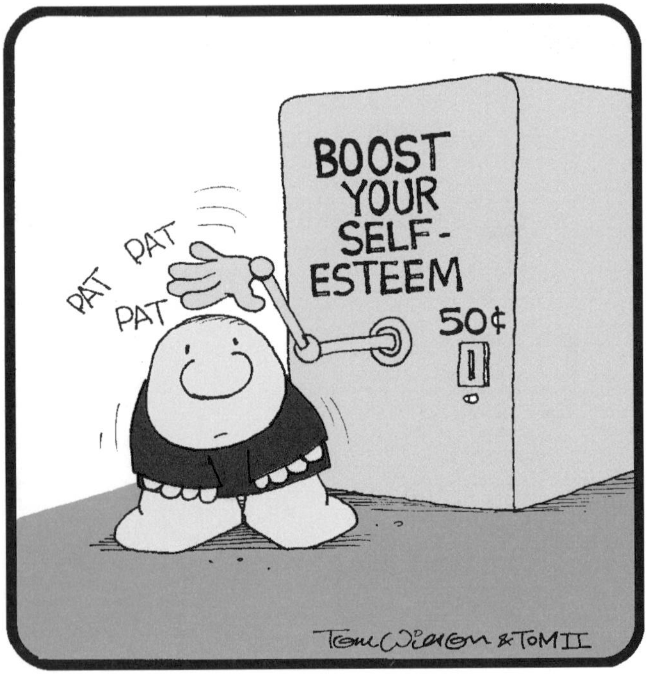
PAT PAT
PAT
PAT
BOOST YOUR SELF-ESTEEM
50¢
TOM WILSON & TOM II

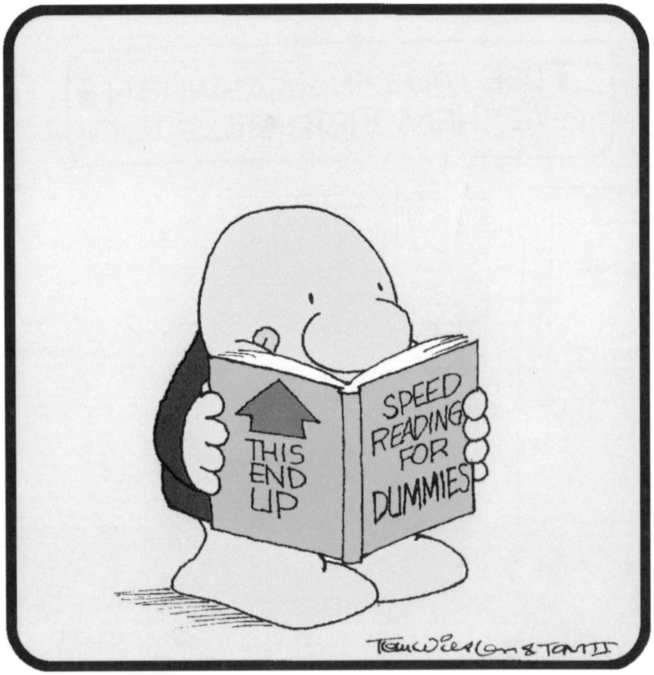
THIS END UP
SPEED READING FOR DUMMIES
TOM WILSON & TOM II

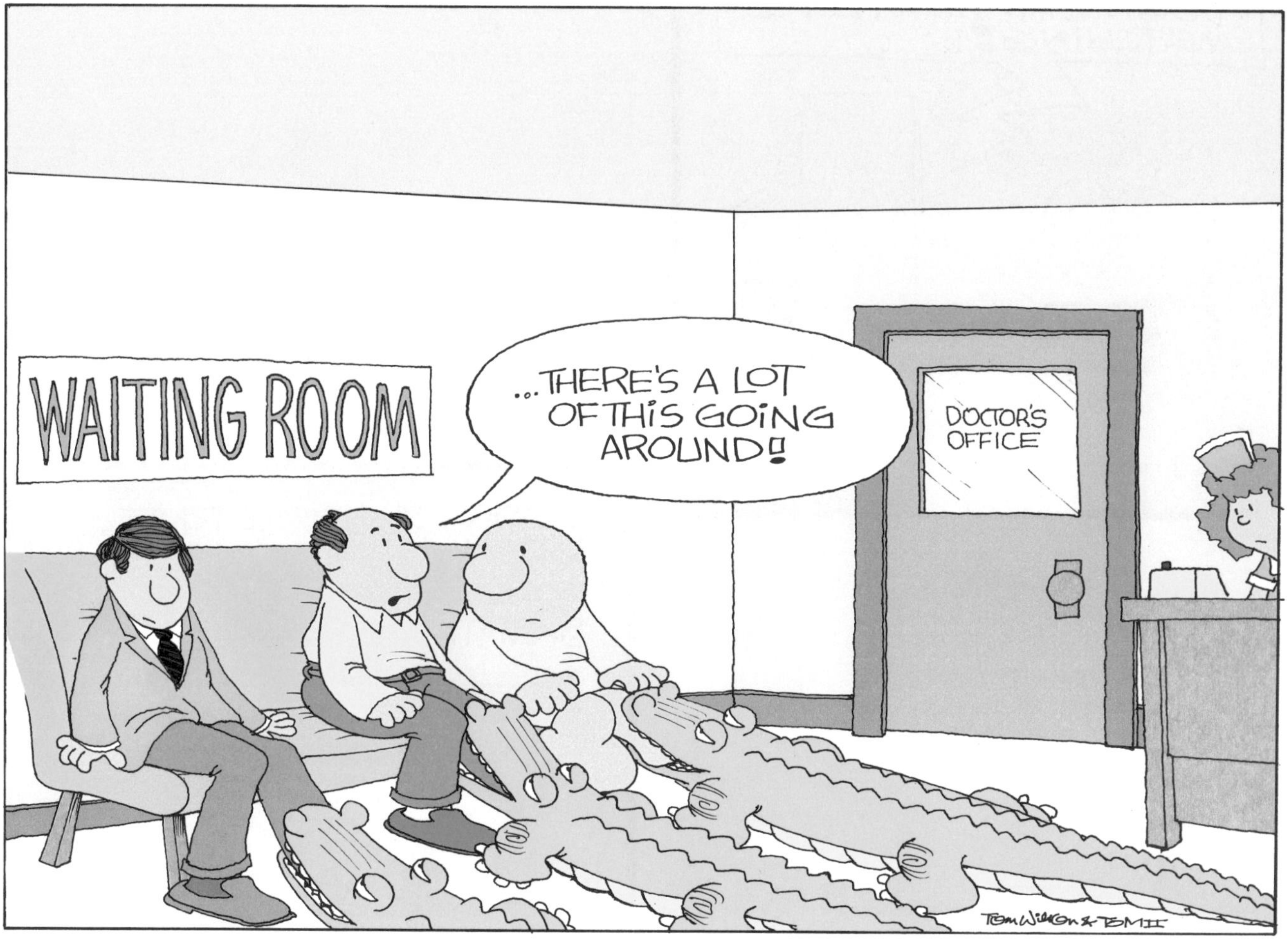
WAITING ROOM
...THERE'S A LOT OF THIS GOING AROUND!
DOCTOR'S OFFICE

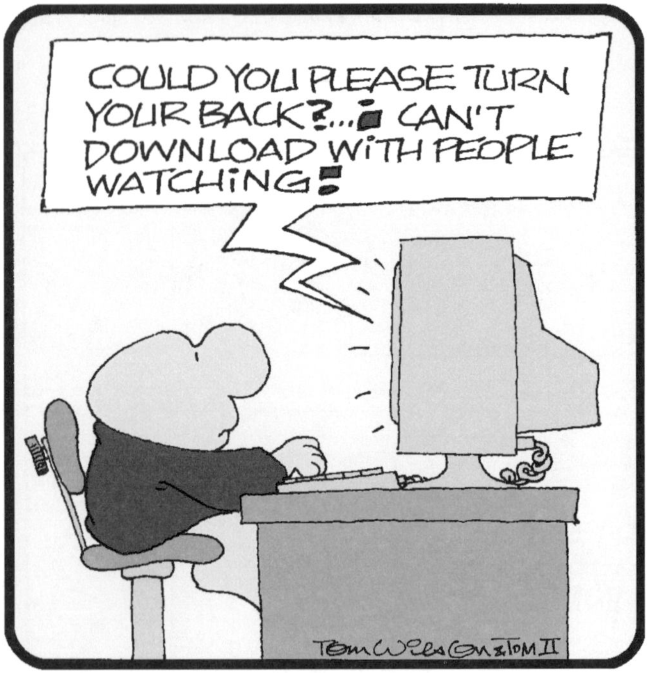
COULD YOU PLEASE TURN YOUR BACK?... I CAN'T DOWNLOAD WITH PEOPLE WATCHING!
Tom Wilson & Tom II

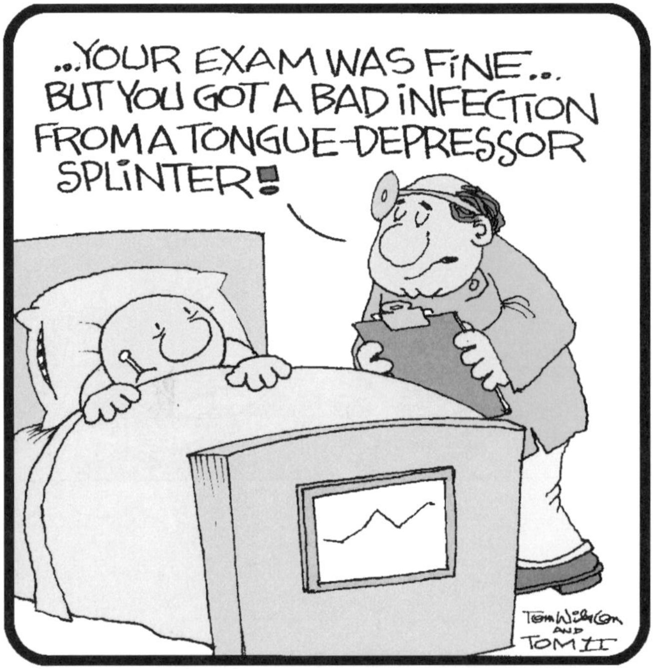
...YOUR EXAM WAS FINE... BUT YOU GOT A BAD INFECTION FROM A TONGUE-DEPRESSOR SPLINTER!
Tom Wilson AND TOM II

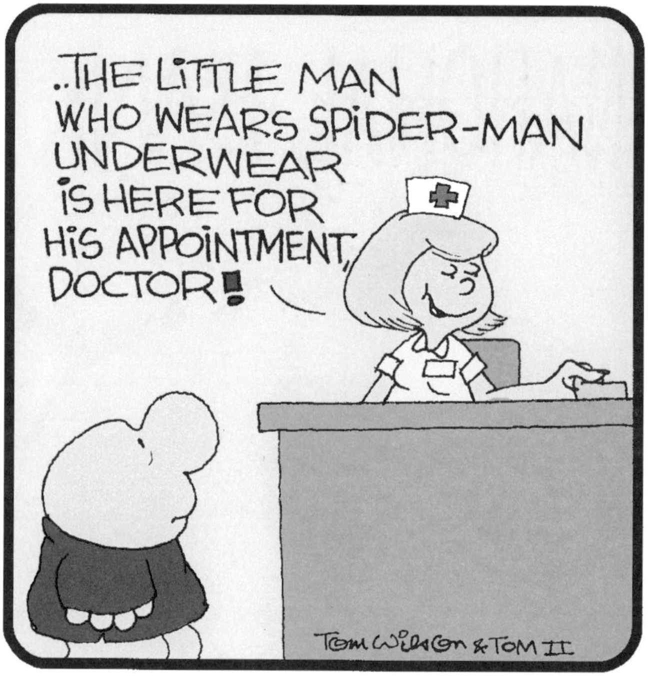
..THE LITTLE MAN WHO WEARS SPIDER-MAN UNDERWEAR IS HERE FOR HIS APPOINTMENT, DOCTOR!
Tom Wilson & TOM II

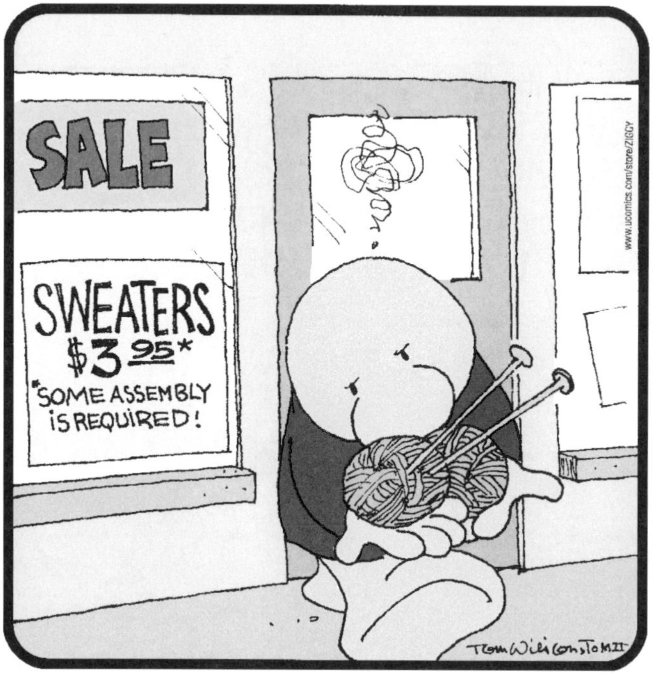
SALE
SWEATERS $3 95*
*SOME ASSEMBLY IS REQUIRED!
www.ucomics.com/store/ZIGGY
Tom Wilson, TOM II

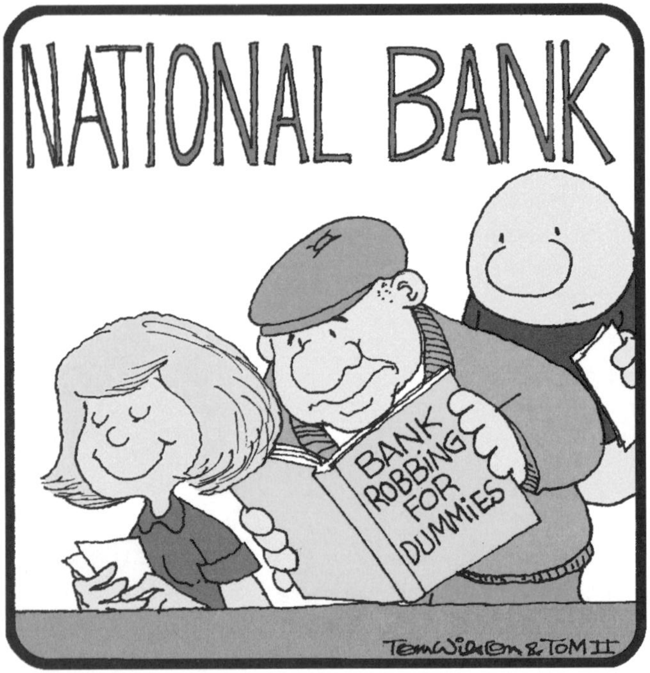
NATIONAL BANK
BANK ROBBING FOR DUMMIES
TOM WILSON & TOM II

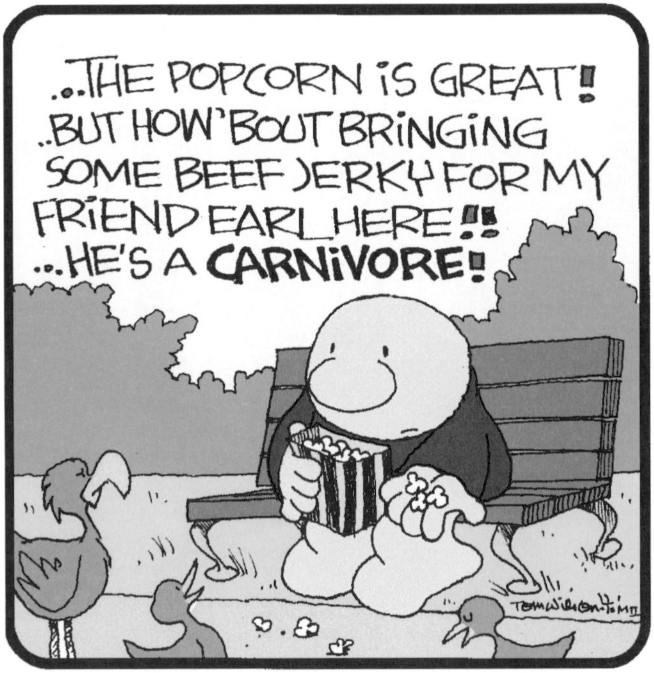
..THE POPCORN IS GREAT!
..BUT HOW'BOUT BRINGING SOME BEEF JERKY FOR MY FRIEND EARL HERE!!
..HE'S A CARNIVORE!

HAS MONSIEUR DECIDED?
YES! I'LL HAVE THE TUNA SURPRISE!
VERY GOOD, SIR!
I'LL BE BACK!
TOM WILSON & TOM II

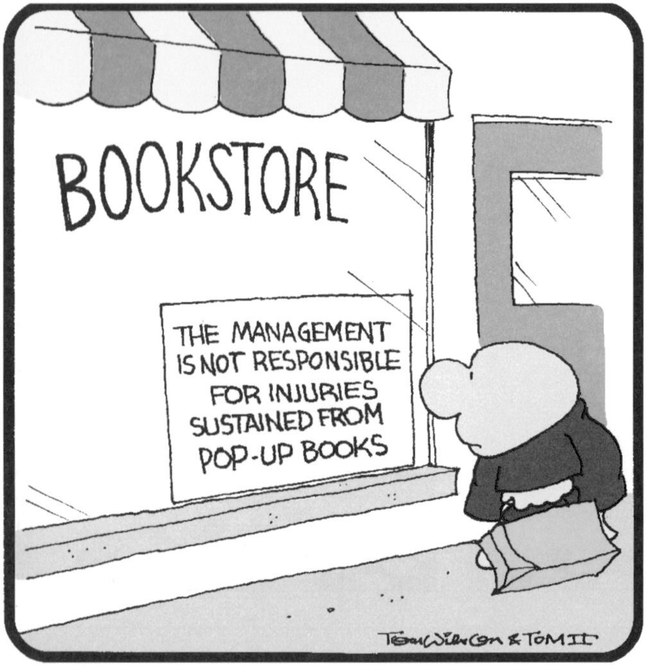
BOOKSTORE
THE MANAGEMENT IS NOT RESPONSIBLE FOR INJURIES SUSTAINED FROM POP-UP BOOKS
TomWilson & TOM II

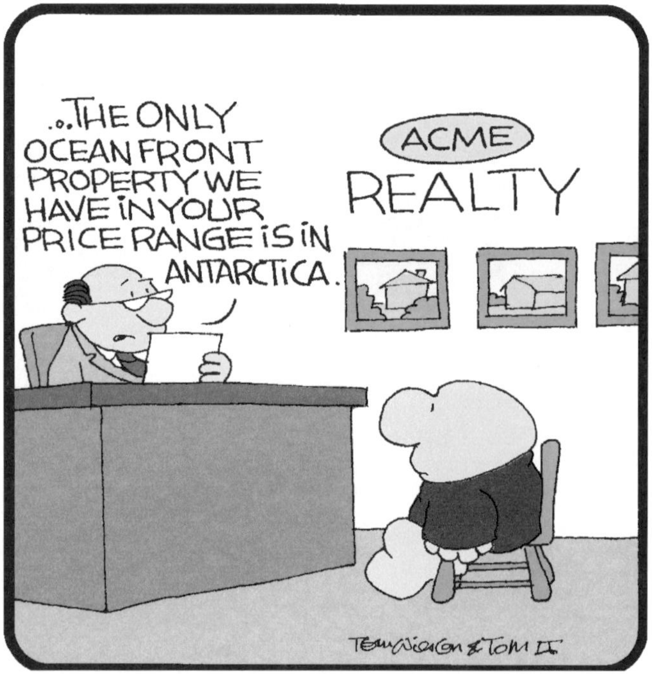
...THE ONLY OCEAN FRONT PROPERTY WE HAVE IN YOUR PRICE RANGE IS IN ANTARCTICA.
ACME
REALTY
TomWilson & TOM II

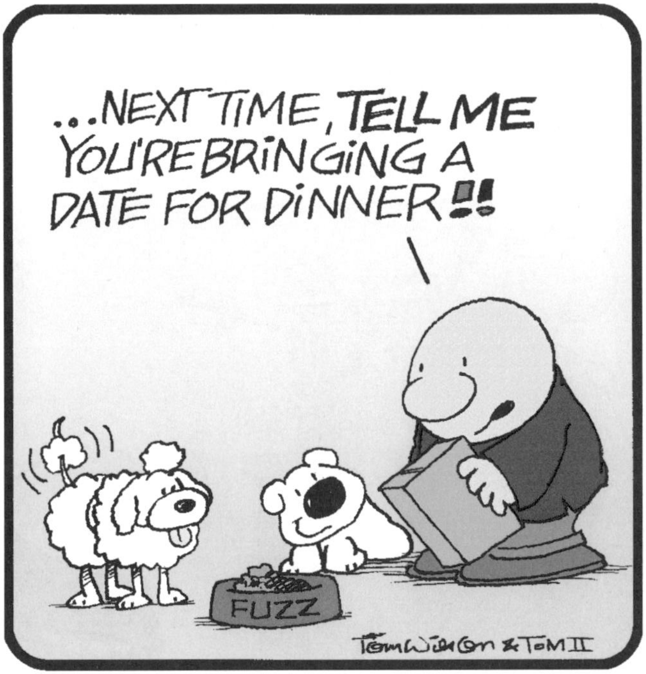
...NEXT TIME, TELL ME YOU'RE BRINGING A DATE FOR DINNER!!
FUZZ
Tom Wilson & Tom II

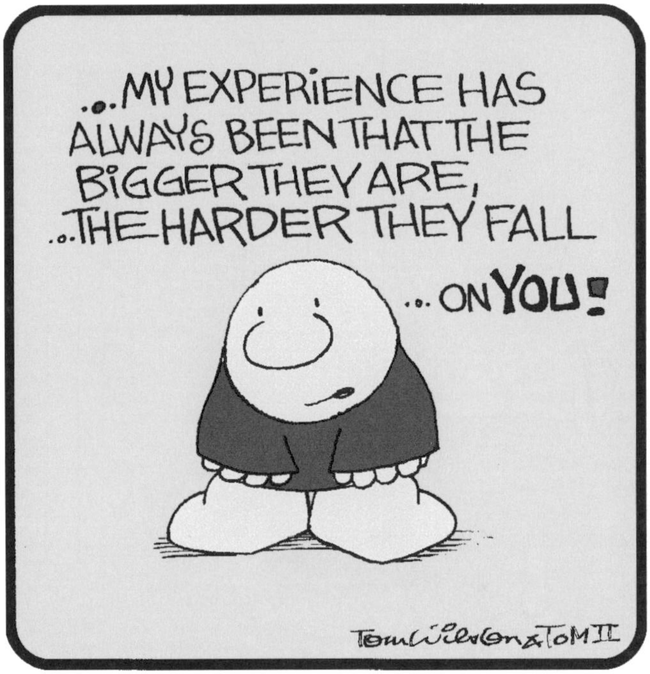
...MY EXPERIENCE HAS ALWAYS BEEN THAT THE BIGGER THEY ARE, ...THE HARDER THEY FALL
... ON YOU!
Tom Wilson & Tom II

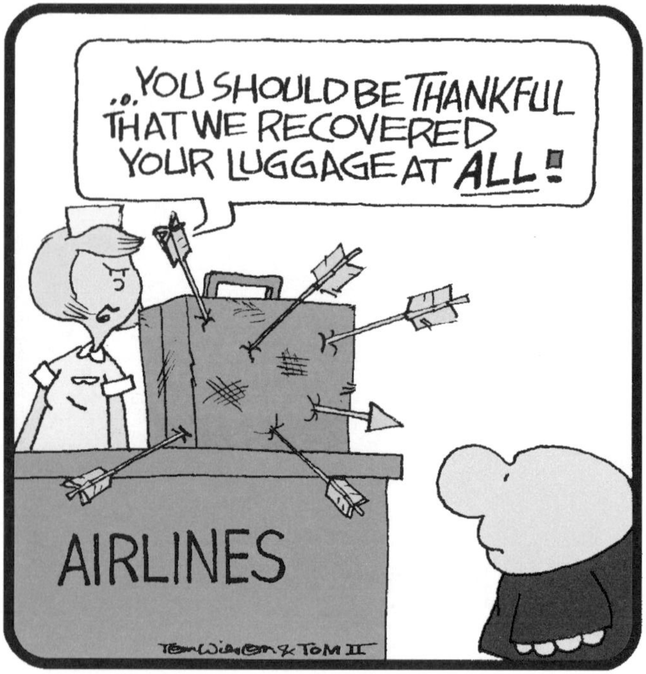
...YOU SHOULD BE THANKFUL THAT WE RECOVERED YOUR LUGGAGE AT ALL!
AIRLINES
TOM WILSON & TOM II

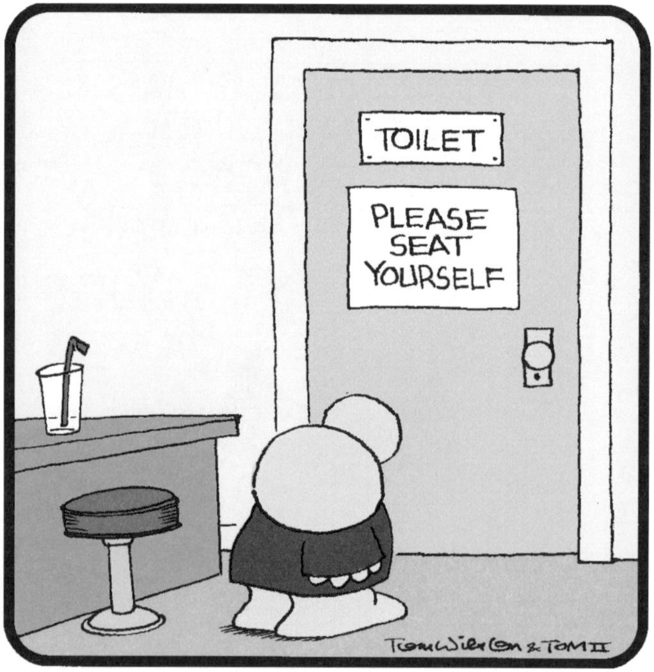
TOILET
PLEASE SEAT YOURSELF
TOM WILSON & TOM II

BING YOU'VE GOT MAIL!
RRRRRRRRRR
BING! YOU'VE GOT MAIL!
VRRRRROOOM
PING!
RRRRRRRRRRRR
ZING
BONK
HEY!
I SAID YOU'VE GOT MAIL!

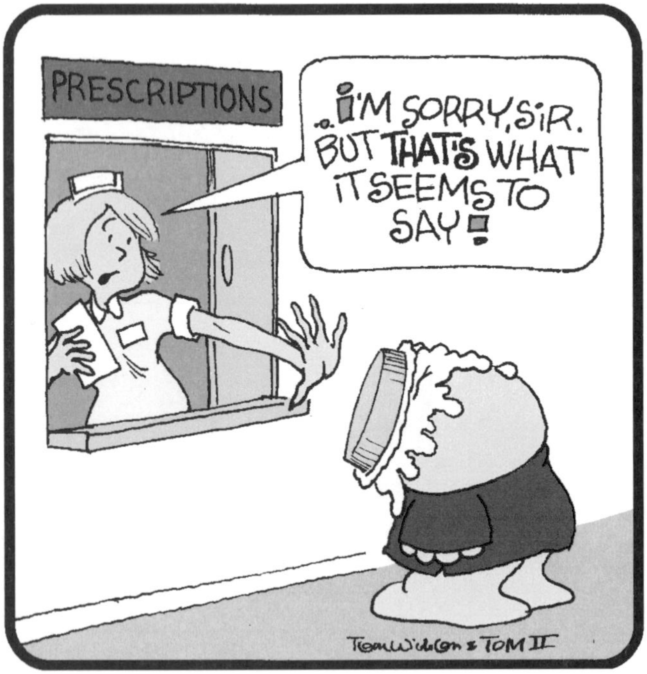
PRESCRIPTIONS
..I'M SORRY, SIR. BUT THAT'S WHAT IT SEEMS TO SAY!
Tom Wilson & TOM II

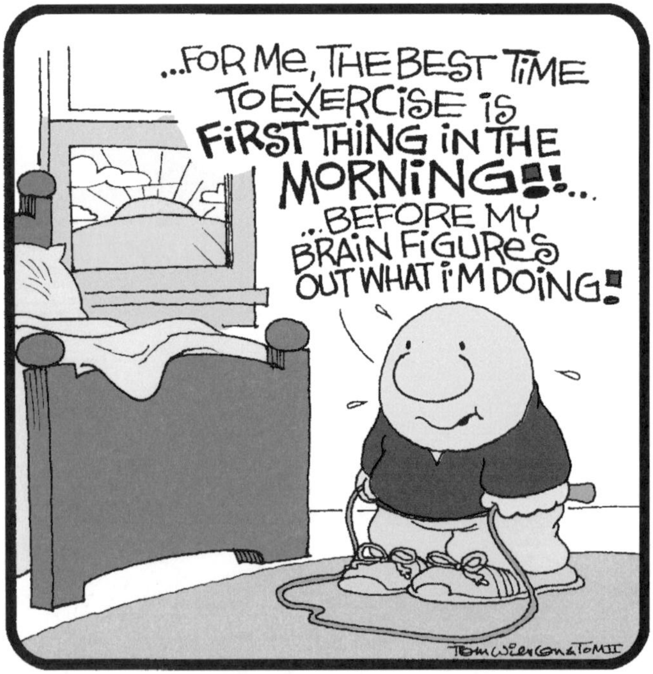
...FOR ME, THE BEST TIME TO EXERCISE IS FIRST THING IN THE MORNING!!... ...BEFORE MY BRAIN FIGURES OUT WHAT I'M DOING!
Tom Wilson & TOM II

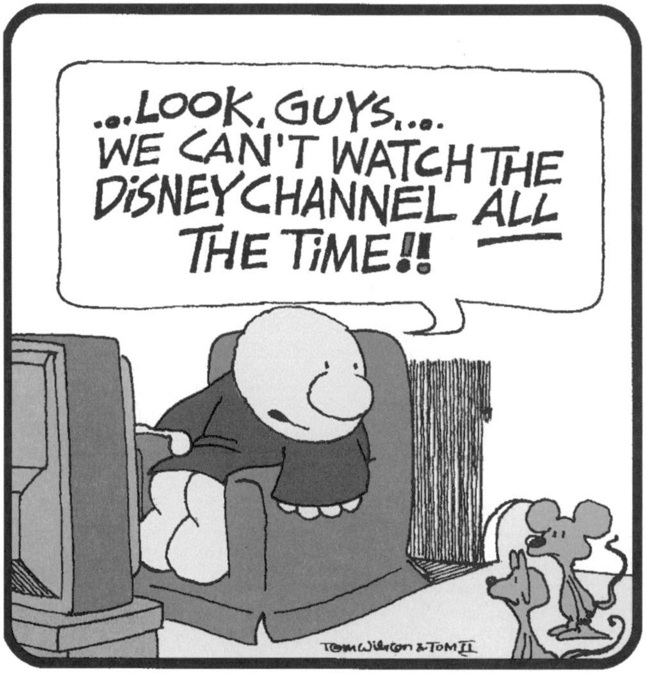
...LOOK, GUYS...
WE CAN'T WATCH THE DISNEY CHANNEL ALL THE TIME!!
TOM WILSON & TOM II

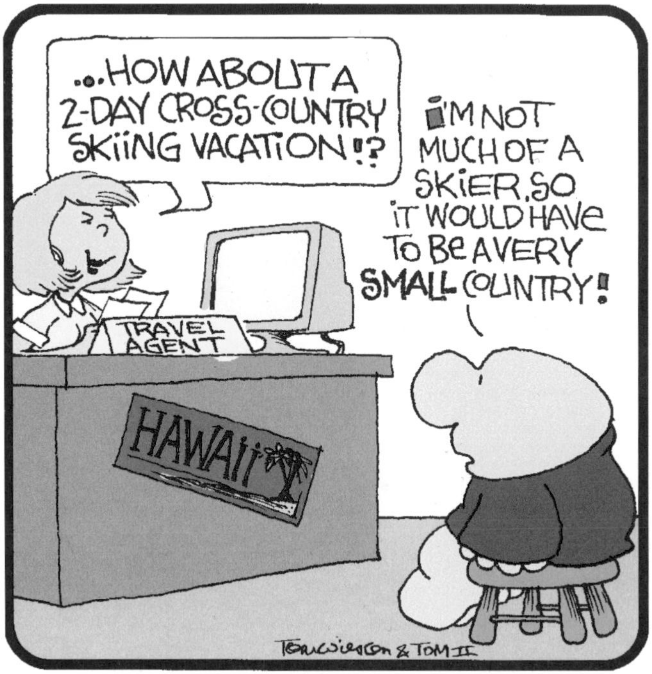
...HOW ABOUT A 2-DAY CROSS-COUNTRY SKIING VACATION!?
I'M NOT MUCH OF A SKIER, SO IT WOULD HAVE TO BE A VERY SMALL COUNTRY!
TRAVEL AGENT
HAWAII
TOM WILSON & TOM II

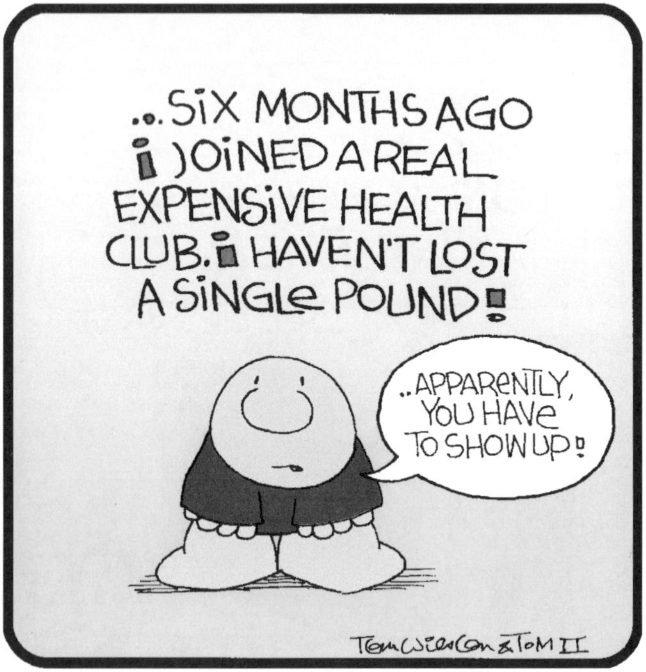
..SIX MONTHS AGO I JOINED A REAL EXPENSIVE HEALTH CLUB. I HAVEN'T LOST A SINGLE POUND!
..APPARENTLY, YOU HAVE TO SHOW UP!
Tom Wilson & Tom II

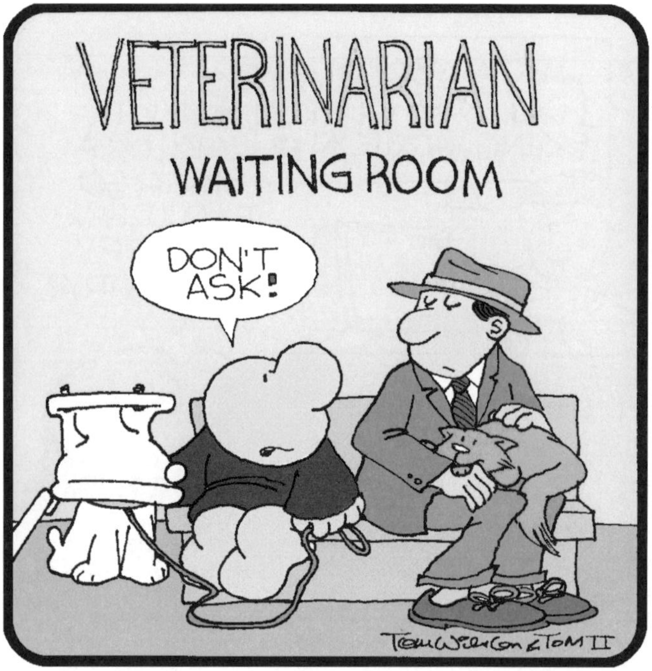
VETERINARIAN
WAITING ROOM
DON'T ASK!
Tom Wilson & Tom II

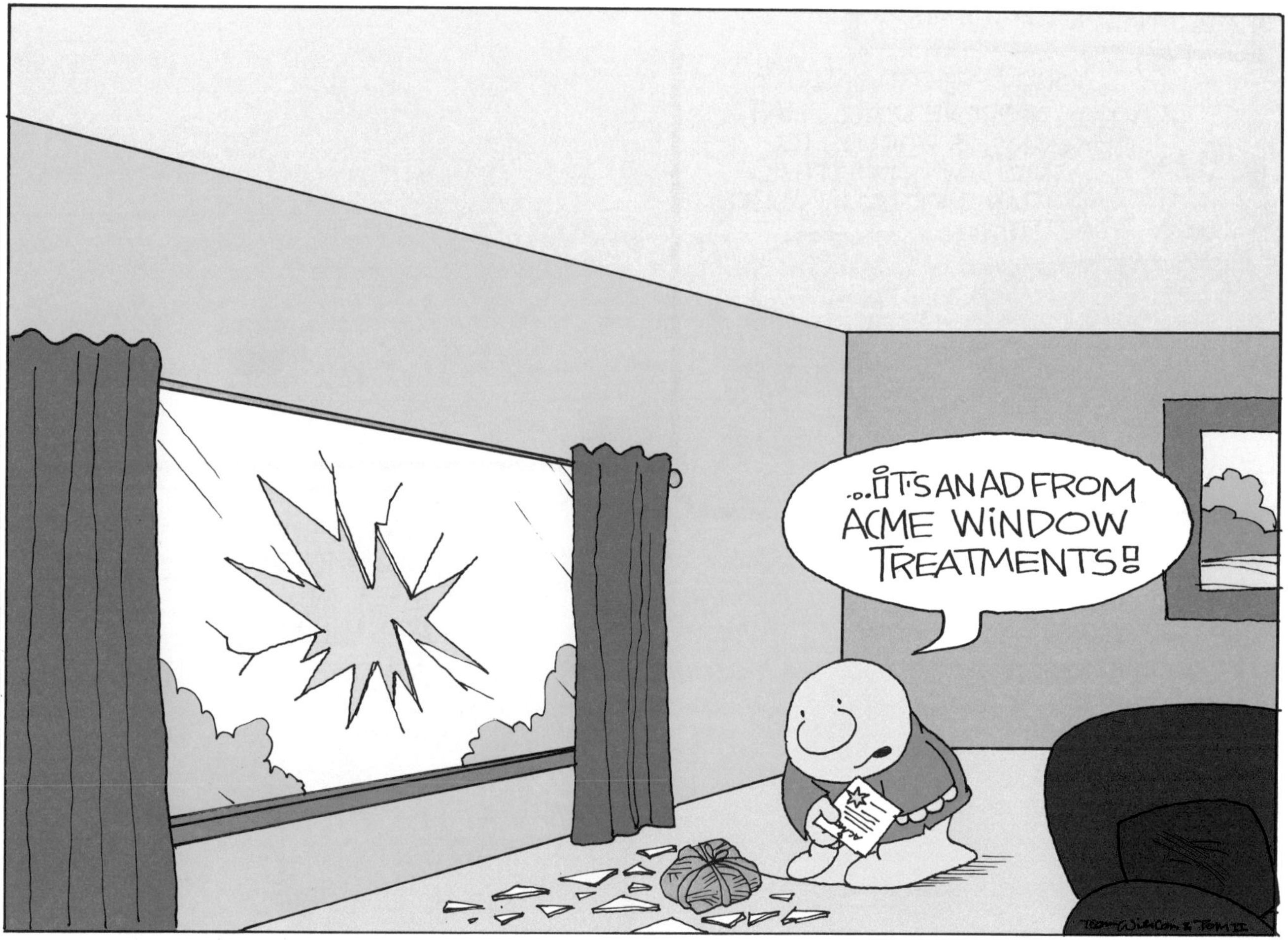
...IT'S AN AD FROM ACME WINDOW TREATMENTS!

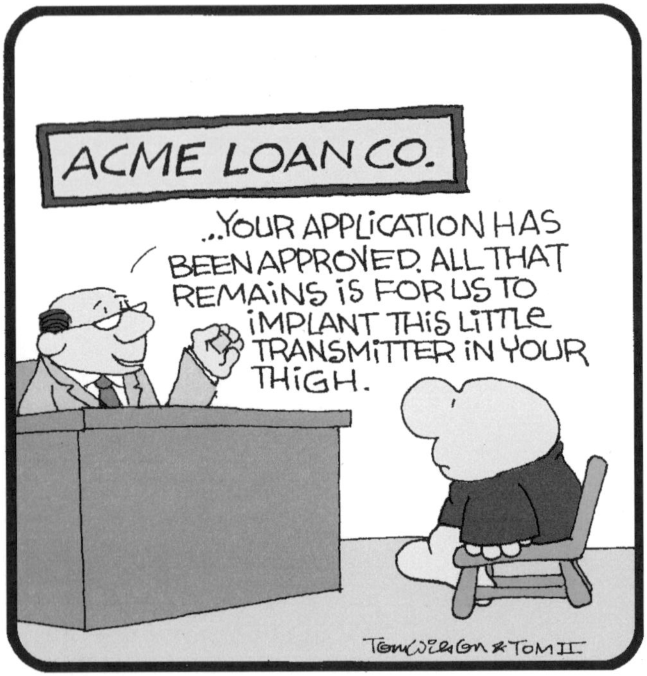
ACME LOAN CO.
...YOUR APPLICATION HAS BEEN APPROVED. ALL THAT REMAINS IS FOR US TO IMPLANT THIS LITTLE TRANSMITTER IN YOUR THIGH.

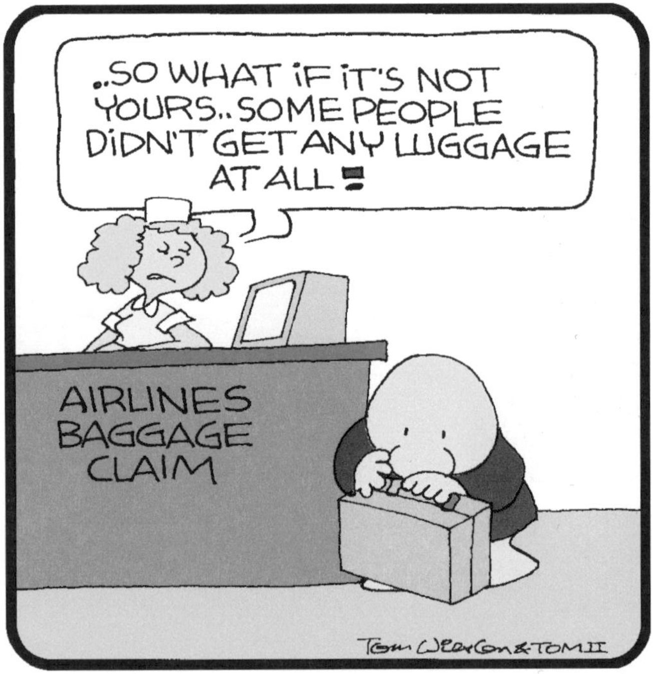
..SO WHAT IF IT'S NOT YOURS.. SOME PEOPLE DIDN'T GET ANY LUGGAGE AT ALL!
AIRLINES BAGGAGE CLAIM

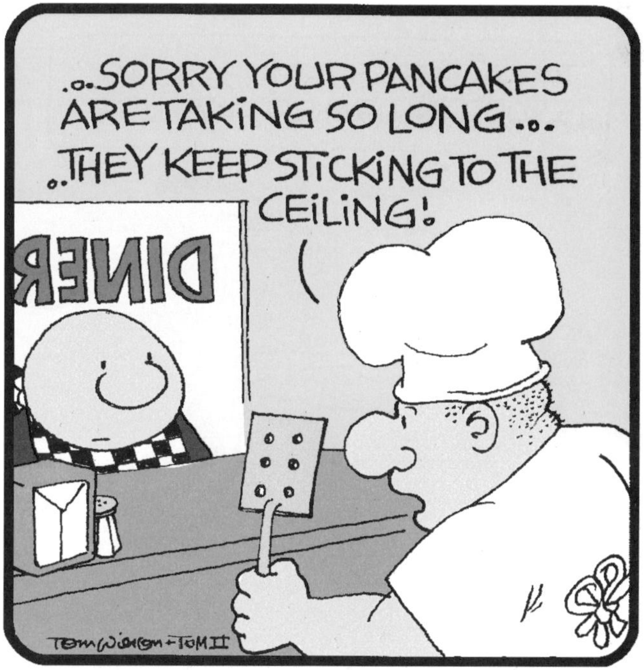
..SORRY YOUR PANCAKES ARE TAKING SO LONG...
..THEY KEEP STICKING TO THE CEILING!
DINER
TOM WILSON + TOM II

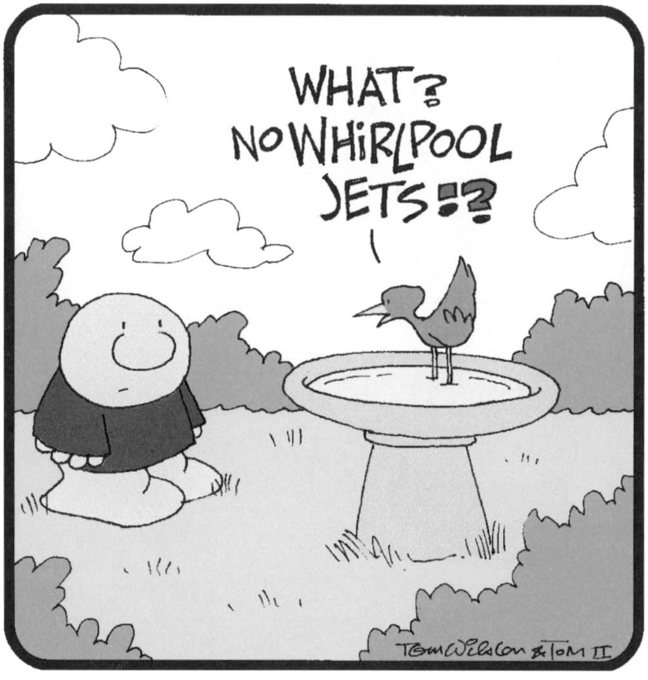
WHAT? NO WHIRLPOOL JETS!?
TOM WILSON & TOM II

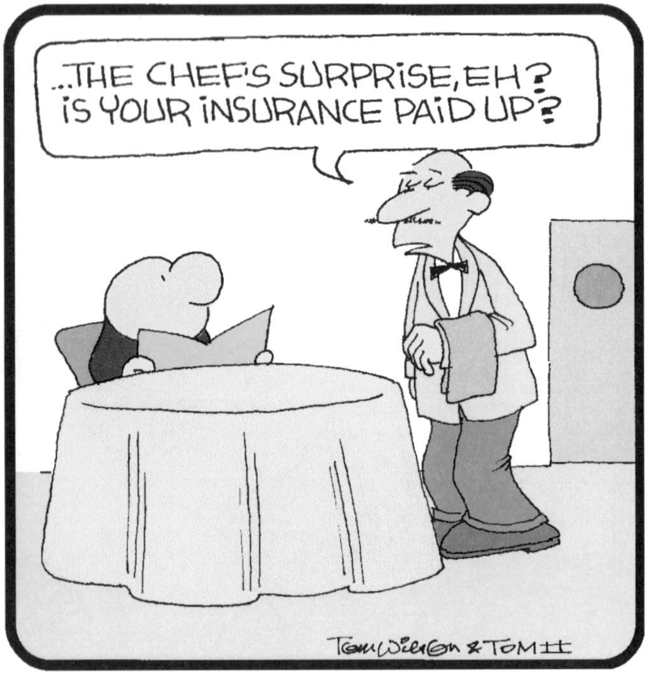
..THE CHEF'S SURPRISE, EH?
IS YOUR INSURANCE PAID UP?
TOM WILSON & TOM II

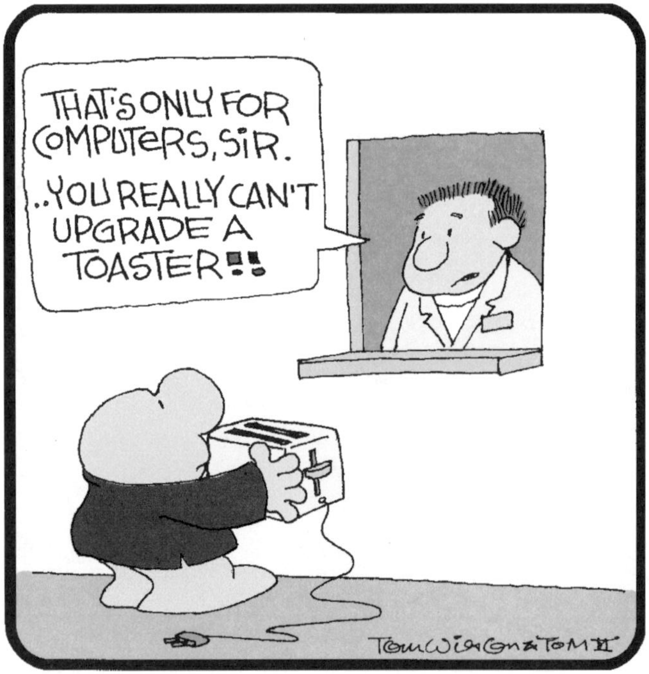
THAT'S ONLY FOR COMPUTERS, SIR.
..YOU REALLY CAN'T UPGRADE A TOASTER!!
TOM WILSON & TOM II

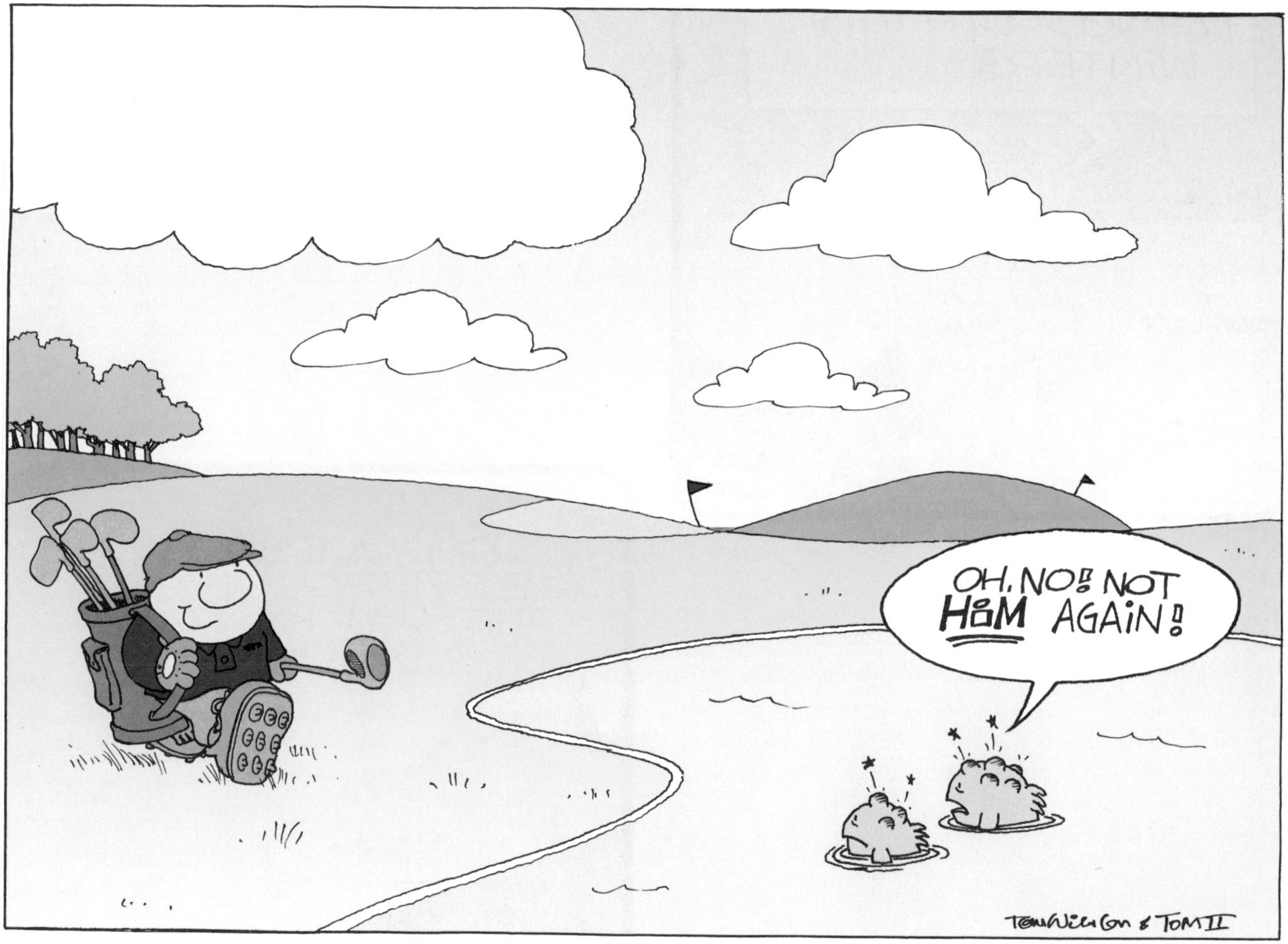
OH, NO! NOT HIM AGAIN!
TOM Wilson & TOM II

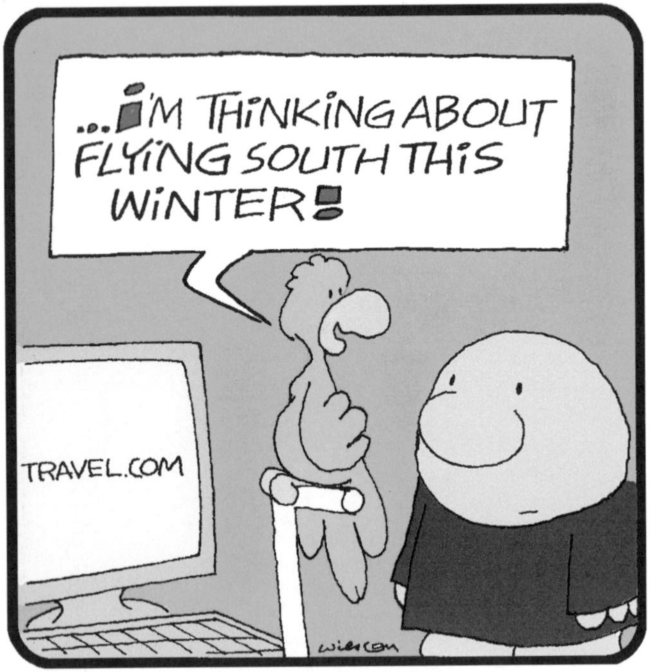
...I'M THINKING ABOUT FLYING SOUTH THIS WINTER!
TRAVEL.COM

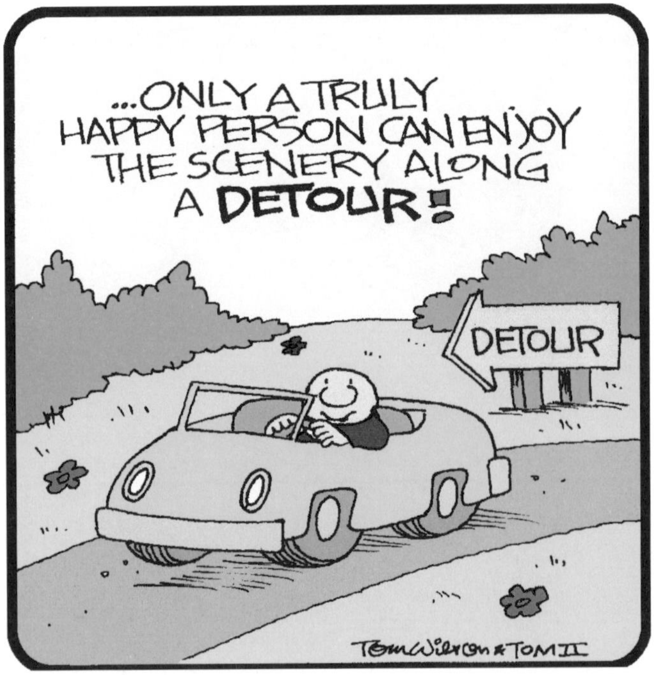
...ONLY A TRULY HAPPY PERSON CAN ENJOY THE SCENERY ALONG A DETOUR!
DETOUR
TOM WILSON & TOM II

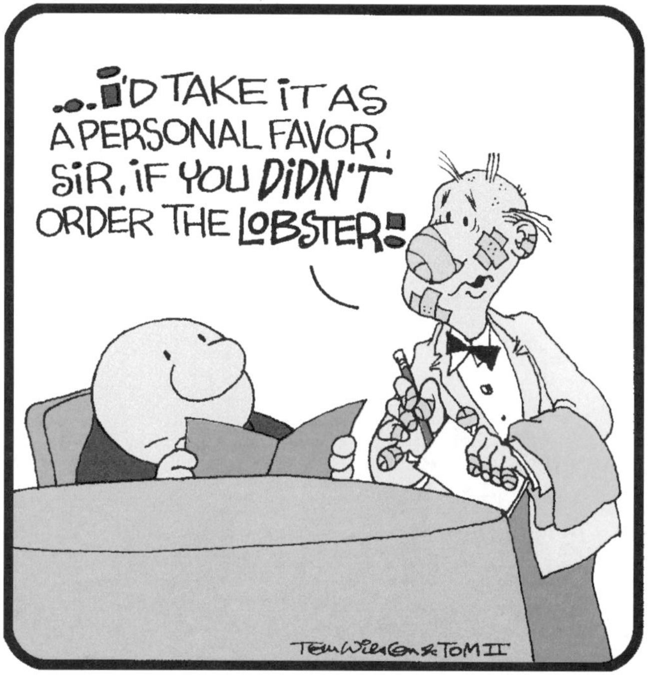
..I'D TAKE IT AS A PERSONAL FAVOR, SIR, IF YOU DIDN'T ORDER THE LOBSTER!
TOM WILSON & TOM II

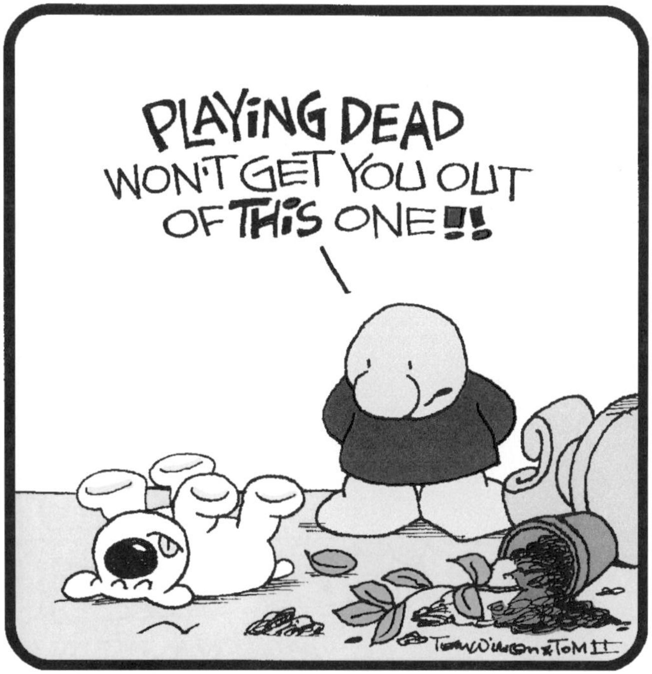
PLAYING DEAD WON'T GET YOU OUT OF THIS ONE!!
TOM WILSON & TOM II

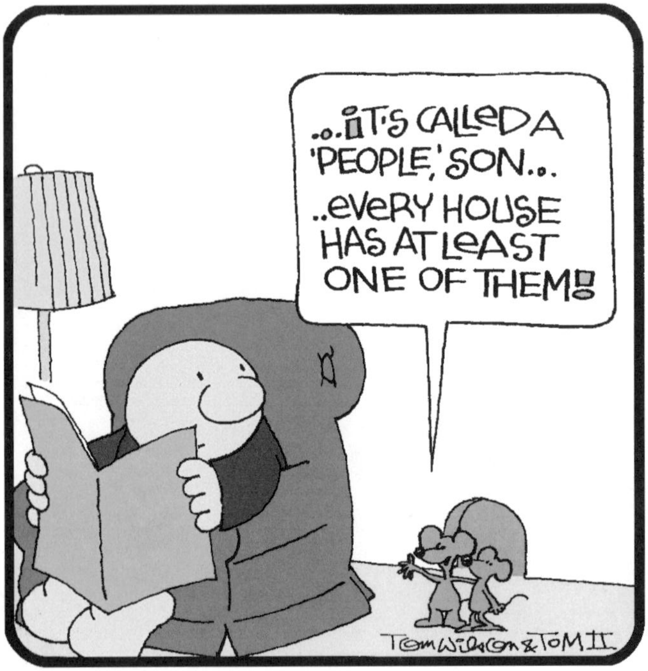
..o..IT'S CALLED A 'PEOPLE,' SON..o.. ..EVERY HOUSE HAS AT LEAST ONE OF THEM!
TOM WILSON & TOM II

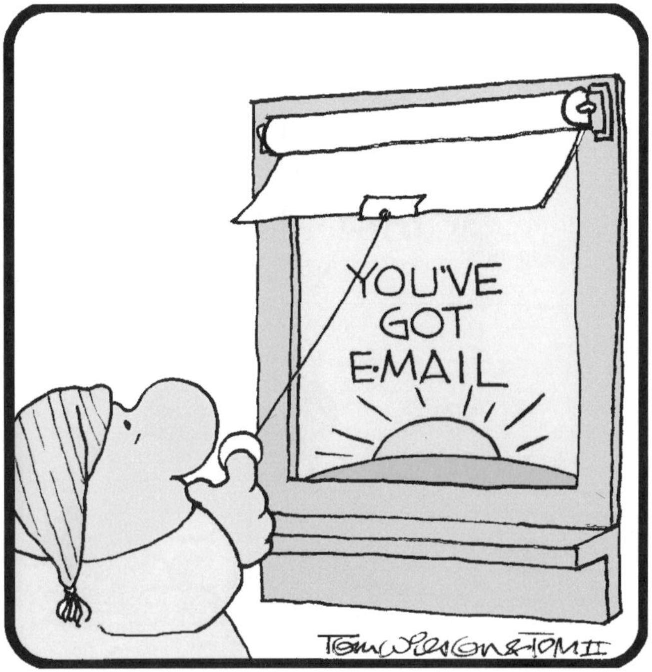
YOU'VE GOT E-MAIL
TOM WILSON & TOM II

...COMING UP NEXT...
'~~CELEBRITY BACHELORETTE~~
FEAR-FACTOR'
CLICK!
...STAY TUNED FOR 'JOE MILLIONAIRE'
CLICK
ANNA ANNA ANNA ANNA ♪ ♫ NICOLE.. ♫
CLICK
...'WHO WANTS TO MARRY AN OSBOURNE'?
AHHHHHH!
..THE TRUTH IS OUT THERE, MULDER.
CLICK
I THINK TELEVISION HAS FINALLY REACHED THE POINT WHERE 'THE X-FILES' IS MORE IN TOUCH WITH REALITY THAN 'REALITY TV'!

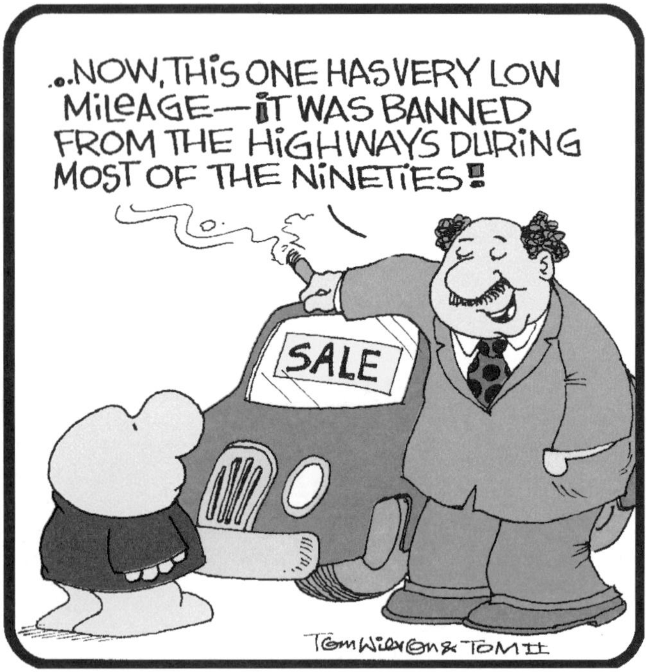
..NOW, THIS ONE HAS VERY LOW MILEAGE—IT WAS BANNED FROM THE HIGHWAYS DURING MOST OF THE NINETIES!
SALE
Tom Wilson & TOM II

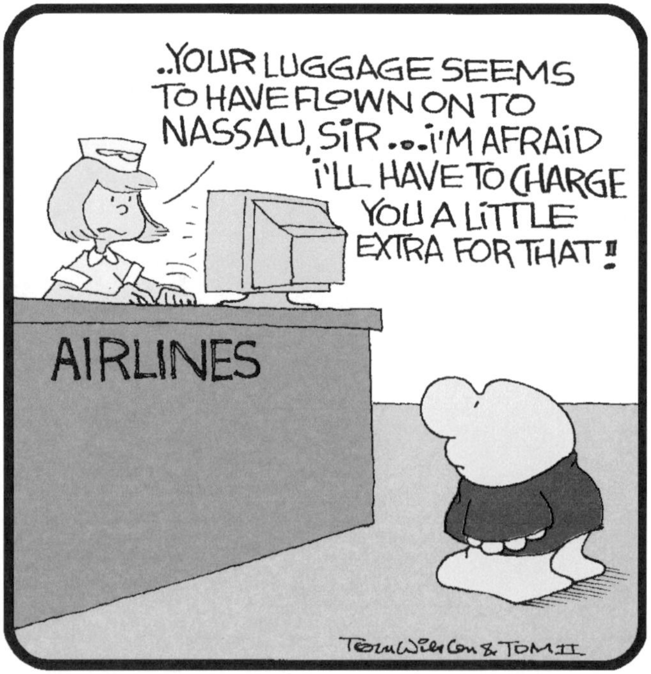
..YOUR LUGGAGE SEEMS TO HAVE FLOWN ON TO NASSAU, SIR...I'M AFRAID I'LL HAVE TO CHARGE YOU A LITTLE EXTRA FOR THAT!!
AIRLINES
Tom Wilson & TOM II

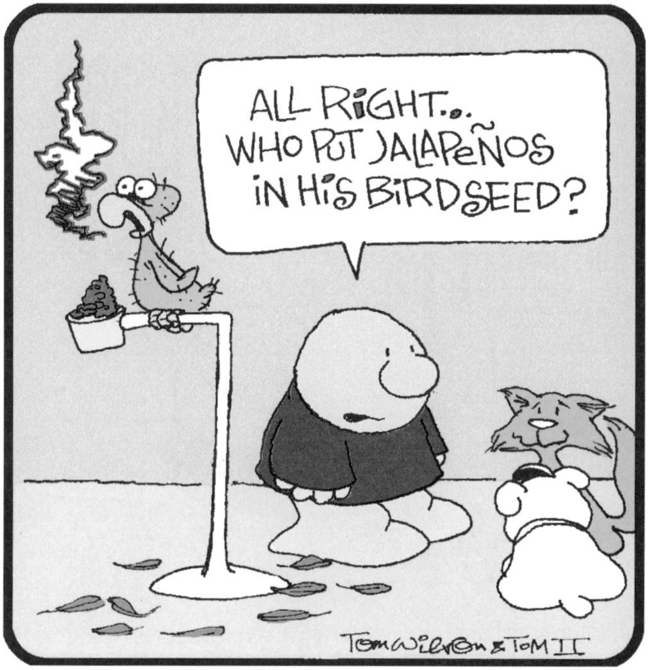
ALL RIGHT...
WHO PUT JALAPEÑOS IN HIS BIRDSEED?
TOM WILSON & TOM II

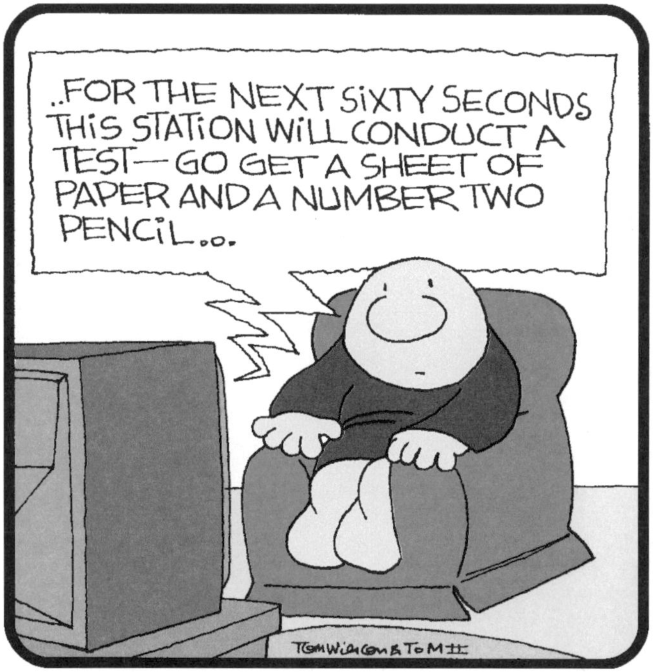
..FOR THE NEXT SIXTY SECONDS THIS STATION WILL CONDUCT A TEST—GO GET A SHEET OF PAPER AND A NUMBER TWO PENCIL...
TOM WILSON & TOM II

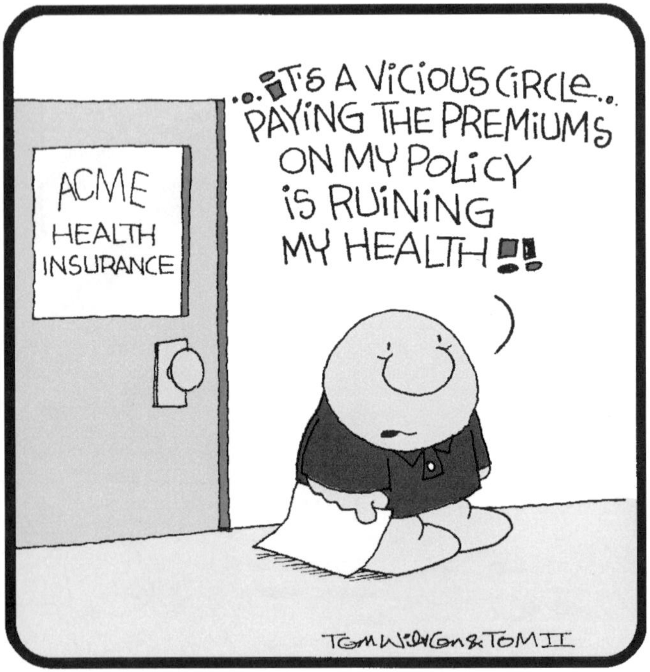
ACME
HEALTH
INSURANCE
..IT'S A VICIOUS CIRCLE... PAYING THE PREMIUMS ON MY POLICY IS RUINING MY HEALTH!!

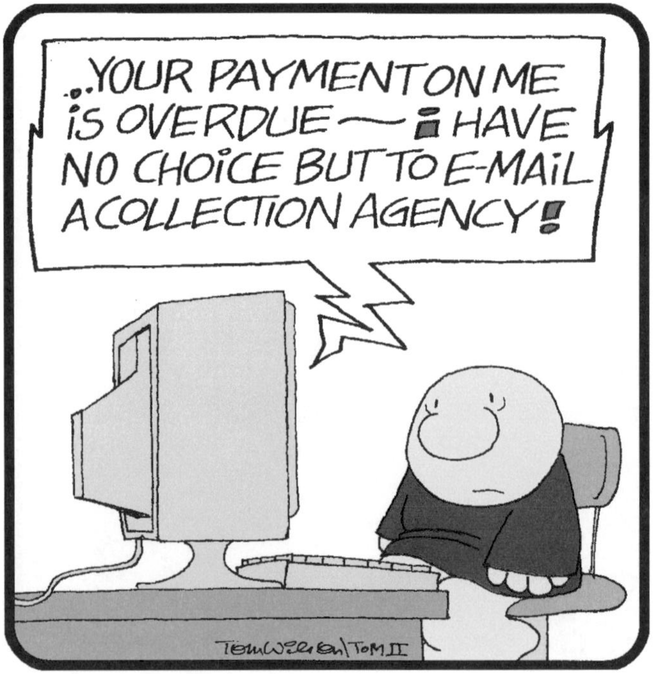
..YOUR PAYMENT ON ME IS OVERDUE — I HAVE NO CHOICE BUT TO E-MAIL A COLLECTION AGENCY!

HUFF...PUFF. HELLO, MR. PENDLETON!
WHY DO YOU DO THAT TO YOURSELF, IGGY!
I READ THAT FOR EVERY MINUTE YOU JOG..
..YOU ADD ONE MINUTE TO YOUR LIFE!
GREAT! IF THAT'S THE CASE, AT THE AGE OF 95...
...I'D GET TO SPEND AN ADDITIONAL 5 MONTHS IN A NURSING HOME AT $5,000.00 PER MONTH!

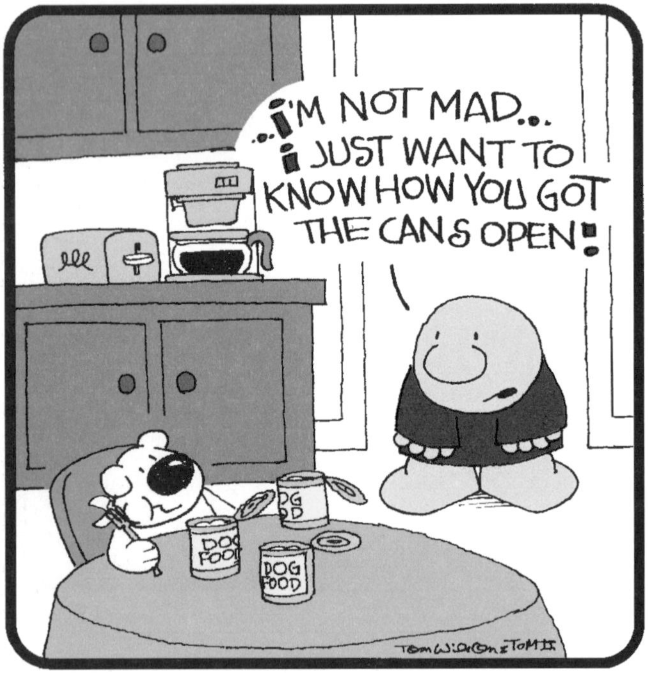
..I'M NOT MAD... I JUST WANT TO KNOW HOW YOU GOT THE CANS OPEN!
DOG FOOD
DOG FOOD

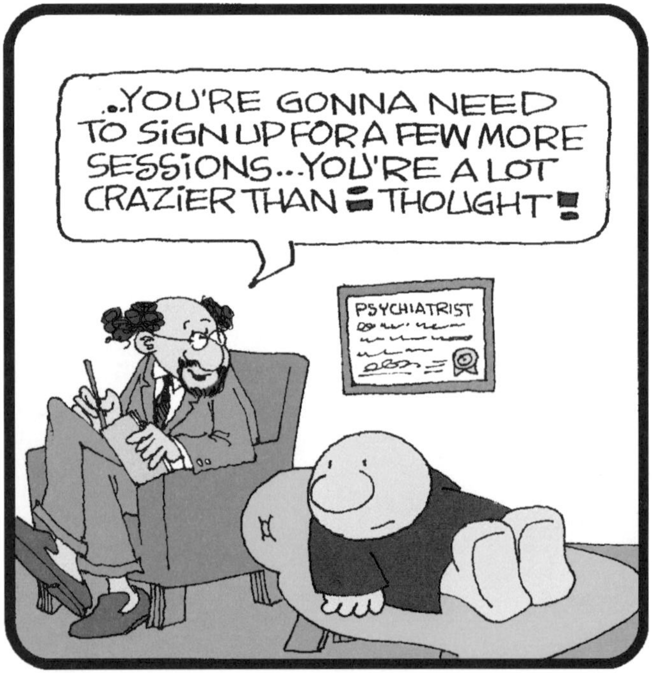
..YOU'RE GONNA NEED TO SIGN UP FOR A FEW MORE SESSIONS...YOU'RE A LOT CRAZIER THAN I THOUGHT!
PSYCHIATRIST

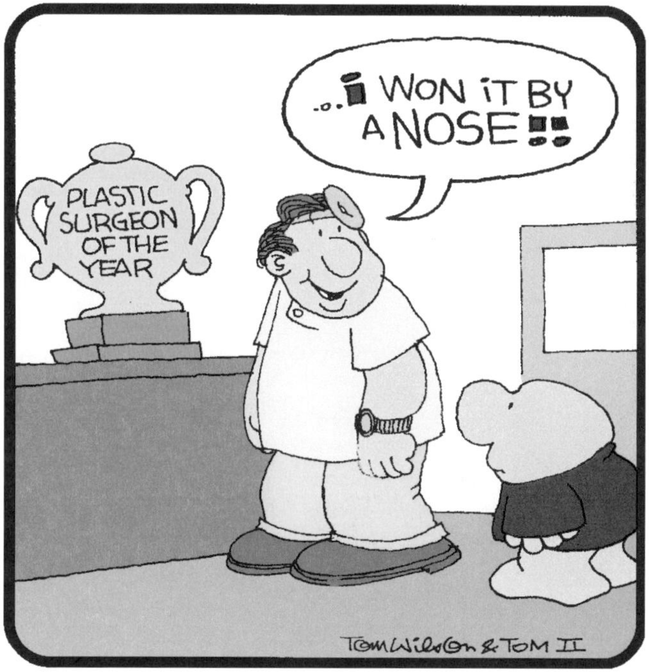

..i WON iT BY A NOSE!!
PLASTIC SURGEON OF THE YEAR
TOM WILSON & TOM II

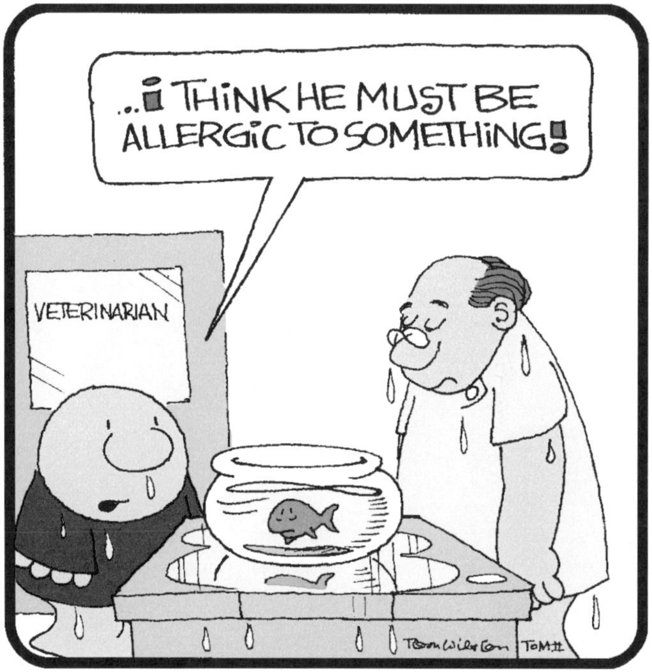

..i THiNK HE MUST BE ALLERGiC TO SOMETHiNG!
VETERINARIAN

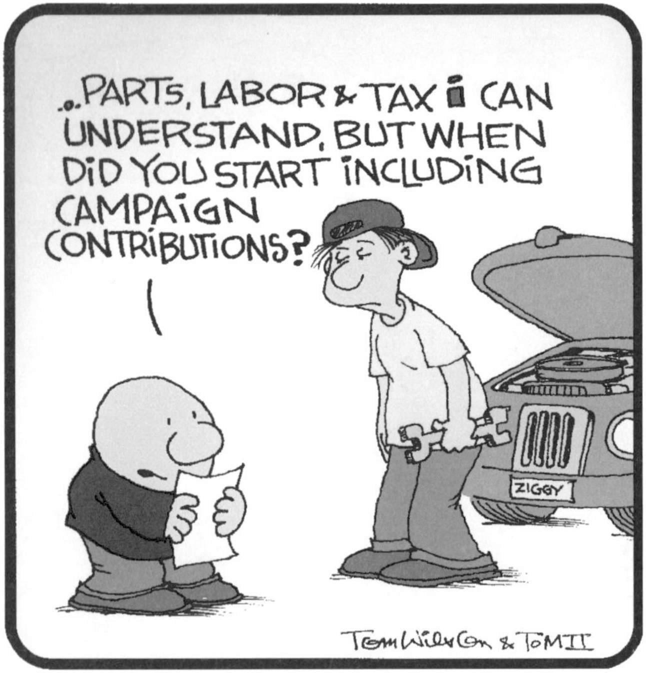
..PARTS, LABOR & TAX I CAN UNDERSTAND, BUT WHEN DID YOU START INCLUDING CAMPAIGN CONTRIBUTIONS?
ZIGGY
TOM WILSON & TOM II

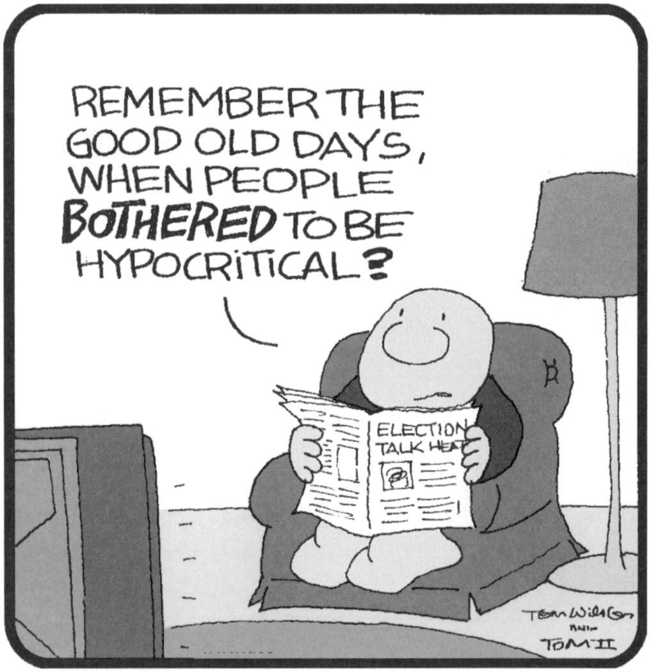
REMEMBER THE GOOD OLD DAYS, WHEN PEOPLE BOTHERED TO BE HYPOCRITICAL?
ELECTION TALK HEAT
TOM WILSON AND TOM II

STARBUX
HELLO!
MAY I HELP YOU, SIR?
STARB
YES!
HMMM..
...I'LL HAVE A CINNAMON BUTTERSCOTCH PRALINE RASPBERRY TRUFFLE LATTE' WITH EXTRA WHIPPED CREAM AND CHOCOLATE SPRINKLES.
...ANYTHING ELSE, SIR?
...A LOW-FAT SCONE!

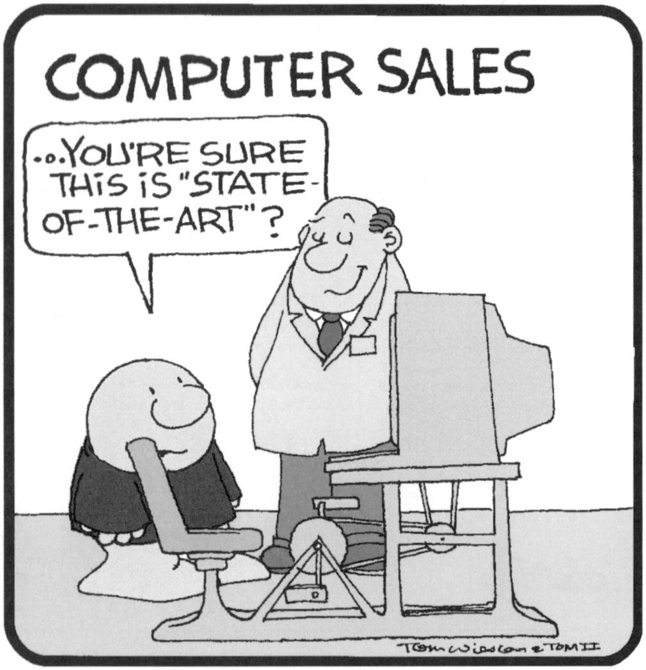
COMPUTER SALES
...YOU'RE SURE THIS IS "STATE-OF-THE-ART"?
Tom Wilson & TOM II

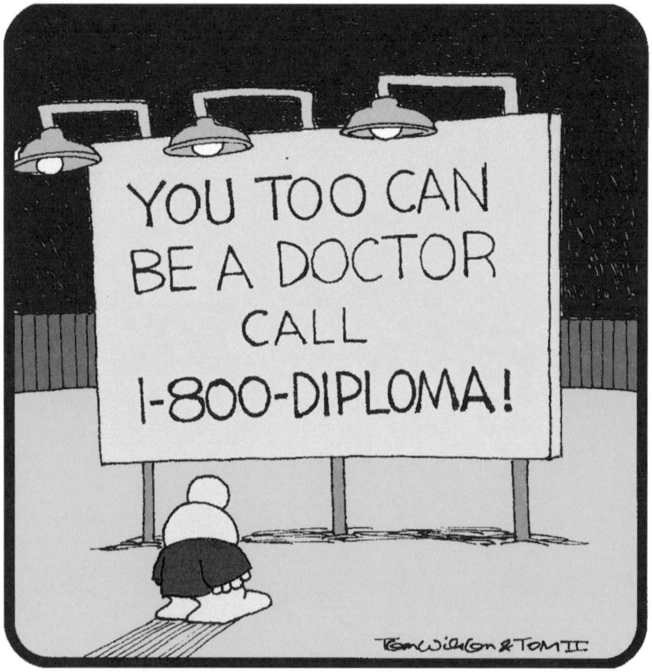
YOU TOO CAN BE A DOCTOR CALL 1-800-DIPLOMA!
Tom Wilson & TOM II

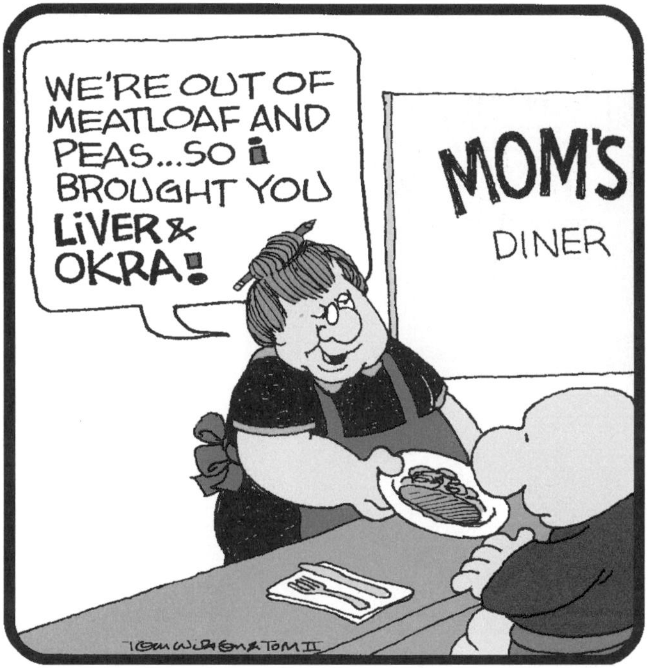
WE'RE OUT OF MEATLOAF AND PEAS...SO I BROUGHT YOU LIVER & OKRA!
MOM'S
DINER

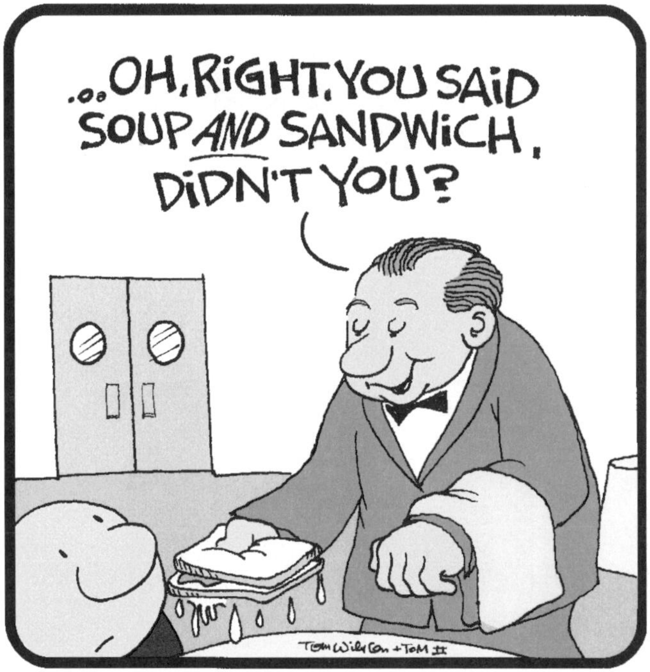
...OH, RIGHT. YOU SAID SOUP AND SANDWICH, DIDN'T YOU?

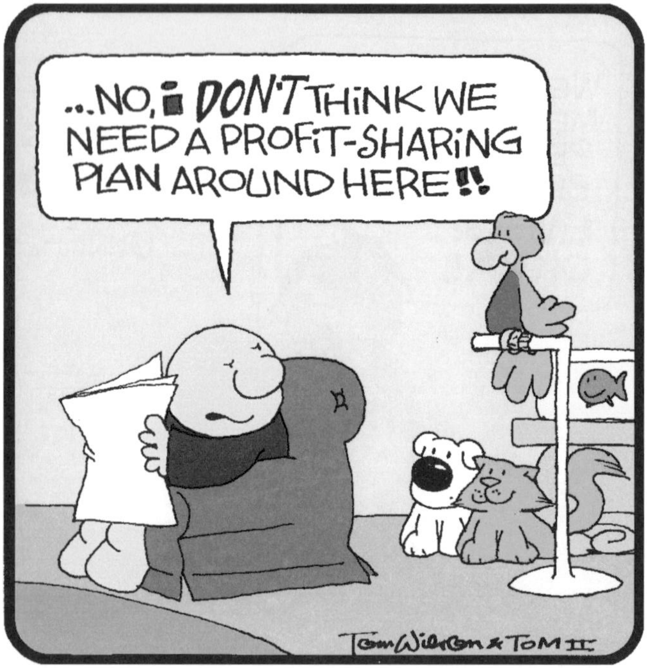
...NO, I DON'T THINK WE NEED A PROFIT-SHARING PLAN AROUND HERE!!
Tom Wilson & Tom II

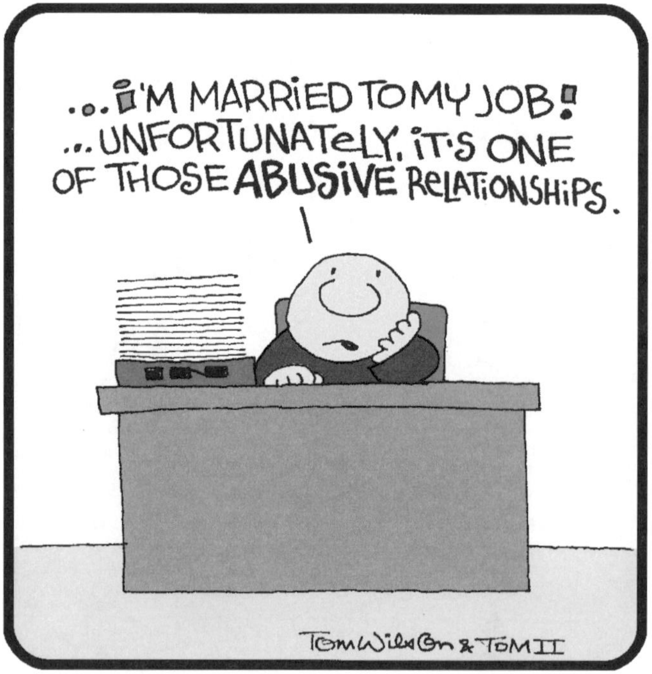
...I'M MARRIED TO MY JOB! ...UNFORTUNATELY, IT'S ONE OF THOSE ABUSIVE RELATIONSHIPS.
Tom Wilson & Tom II

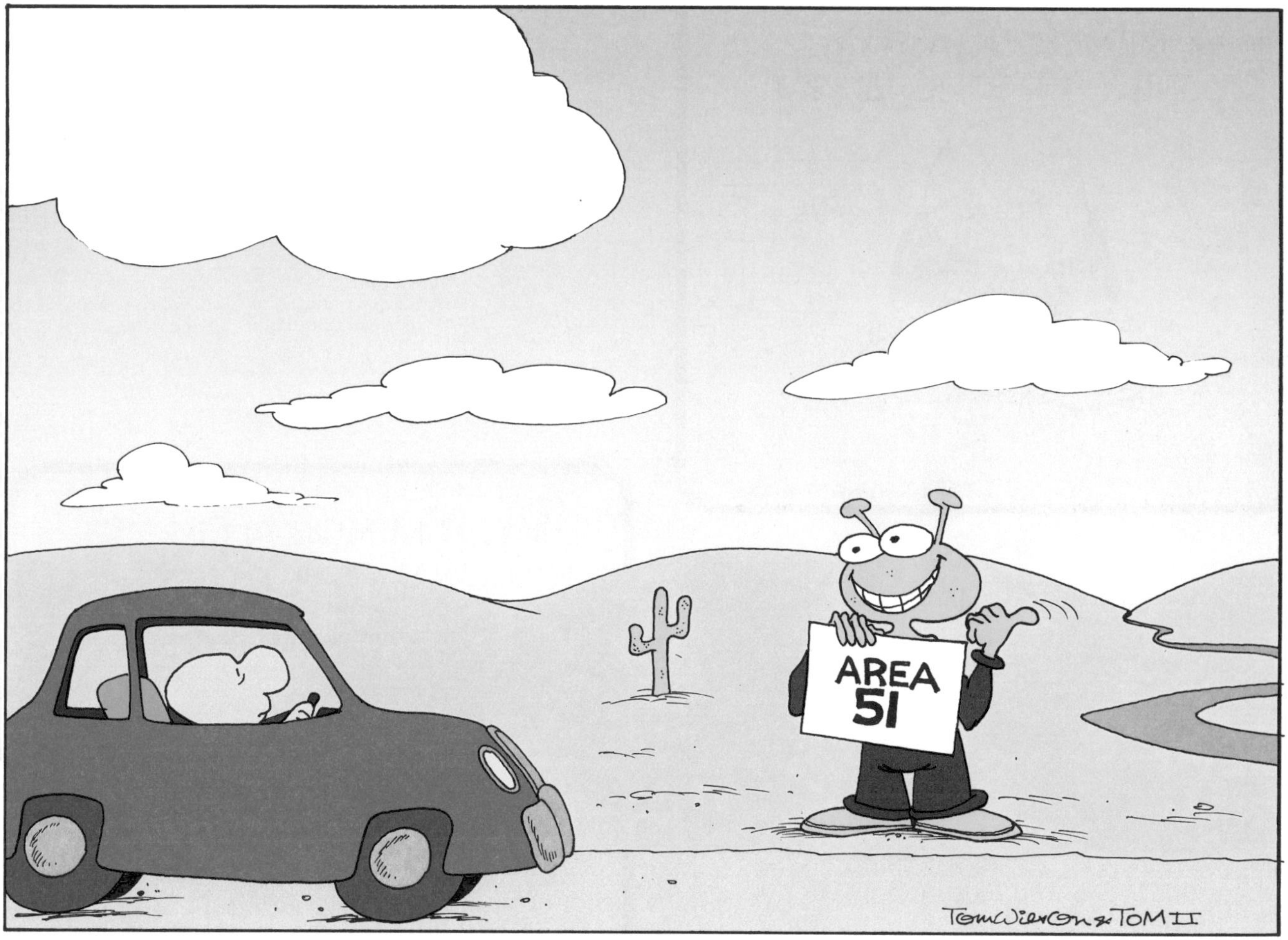
AREA
51
TomWilson & TOM II

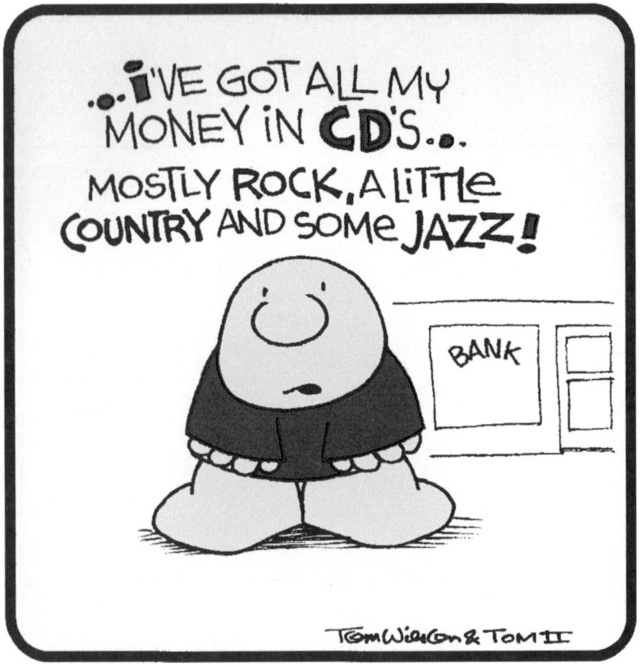
..I'VE GOT ALL MY MONEY IN CD'S... MOSTLY ROCK, A LITTLE COUNTRY AND SOME JAZZ!
BANK
TOM WILSON & TOM II

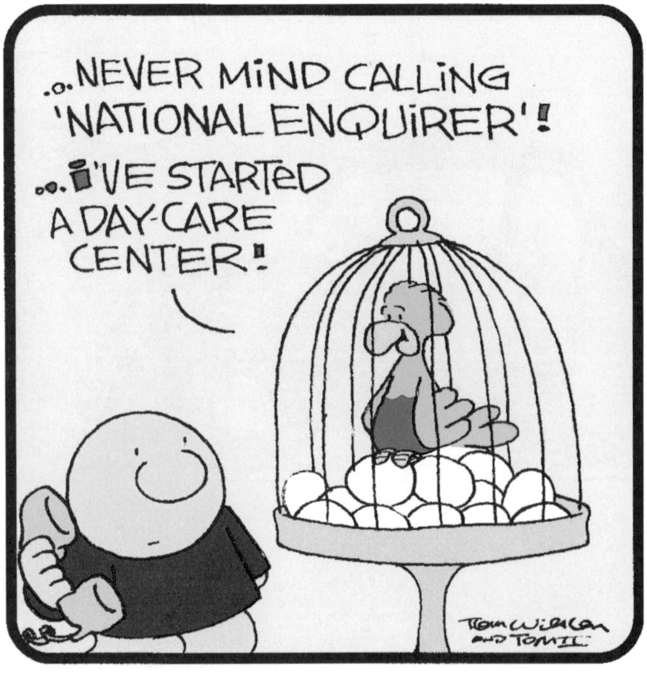
..NEVER MIND CALLING 'NATIONAL ENQUIRER'! ..I'VE STARTED A DAY-CARE CENTER!
TOM WILSON AND TOM II

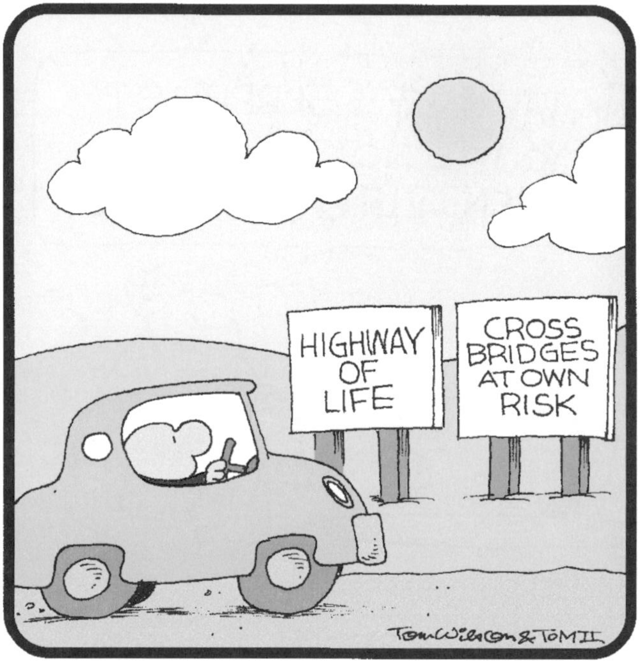
HIGHWAY
OF
LIFE
CROSS
BRIDGES
AT OWN
RISK

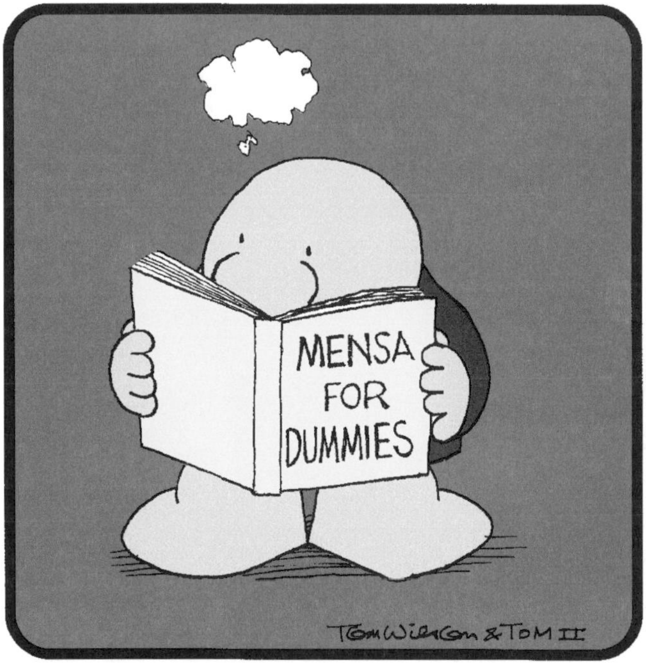
MENSA
FOR
DUMMIES

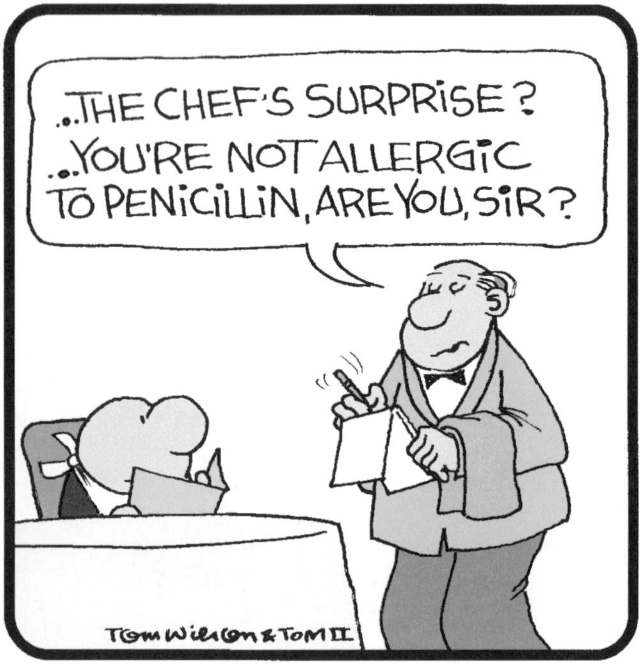
..THE CHEF'S SURPRISE?
..YOU'RE NOT ALLERGIC TO PENICILLIN, ARE YOU, SIR?
TOM WILSON & TOM II

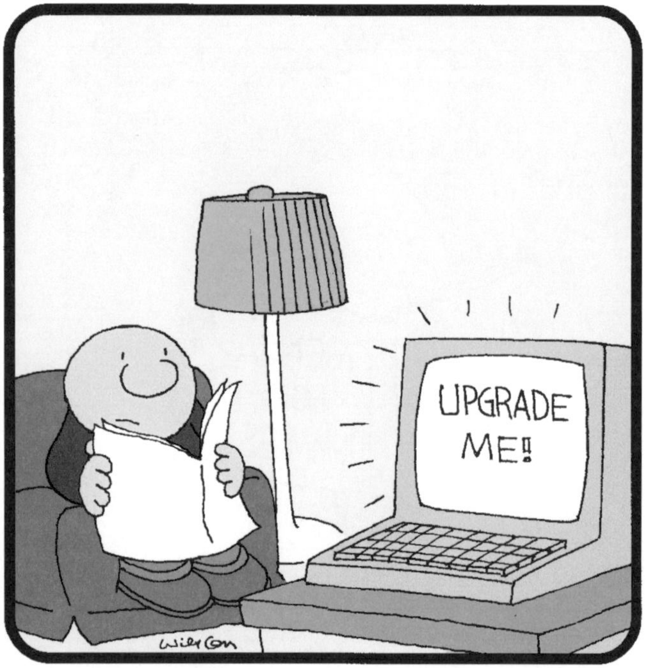
UPGRADE ME!!
WILSON

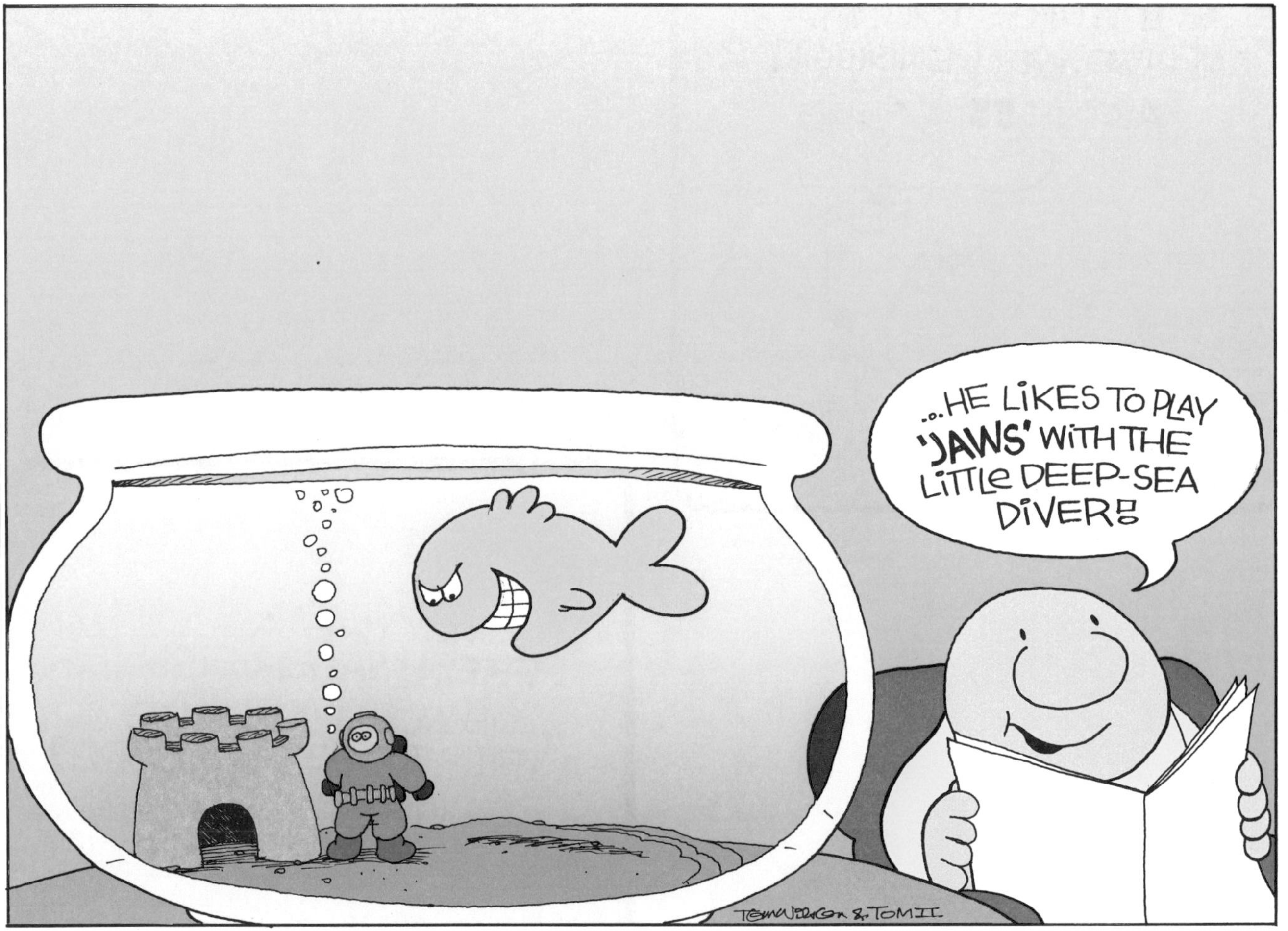
...HE LIKES TO PLAY 'JAWS' WITH THE LITTLE DEEP-SEA DIVER!!
TOM WILSON & TOM II.

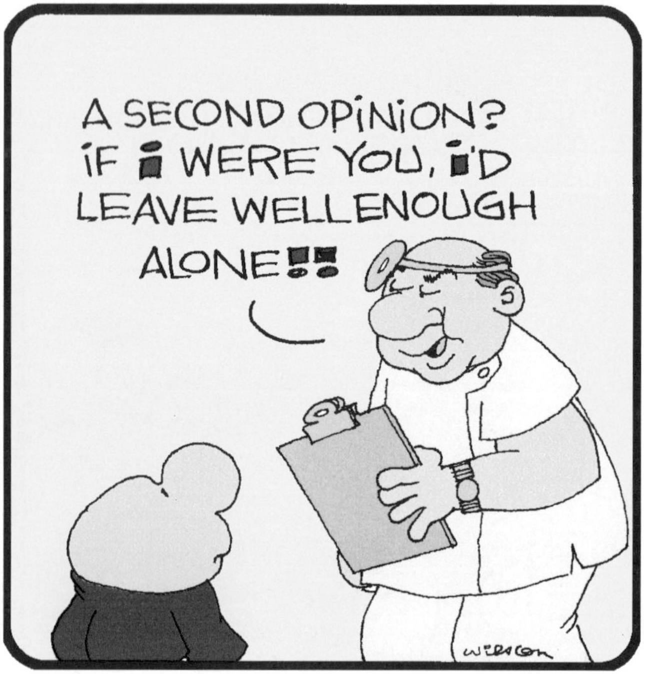
A SECOND OPINION? IF I WERE YOU, I'D LEAVE WELLENOUGH ALONE!!
WILSON

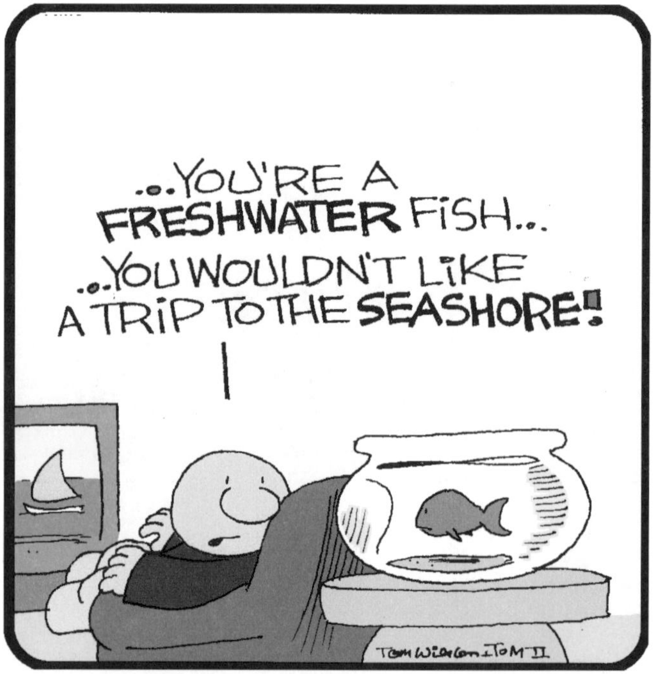
..YOU'RE A FRESHWATER FISH... ..YOU WOULDN'T LIKE A TRIP TO THE SEASHORE!
TOM WILSON I TOM II

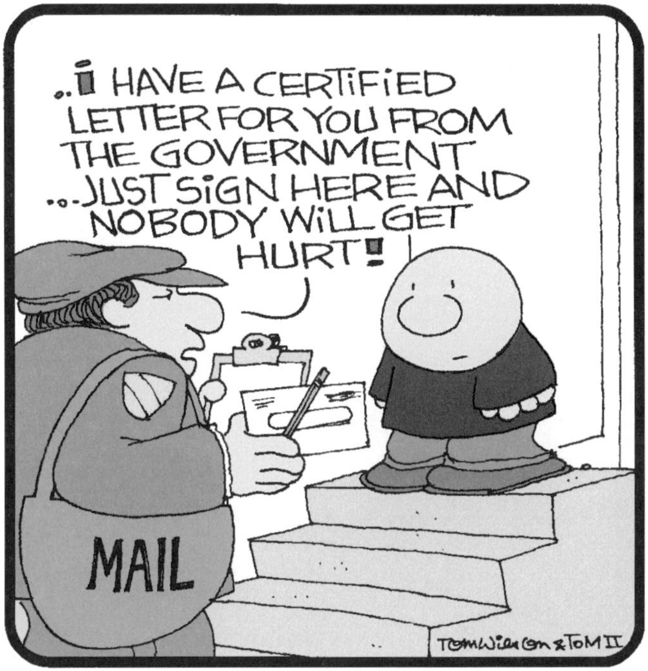
..I HAVE A CERTIFIED LETTER FOR YOU FROM THE GOVERNMENT ..JUST SIGN HERE AND NOBODY WILL GET HURT!!
MAIL
TOM WILSON & TOM II

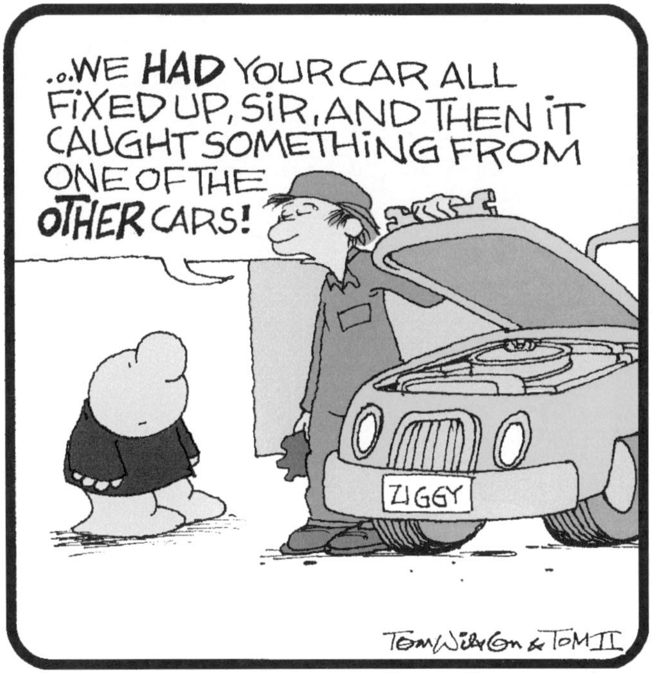
..WE HAD YOUR CAR ALL FIXED UP, SIR, AND THEN IT CAUGHT SOMETHING FROM ONE OF THE OTHER CARS!
ZIGGY
TOM WILSON & TOM II

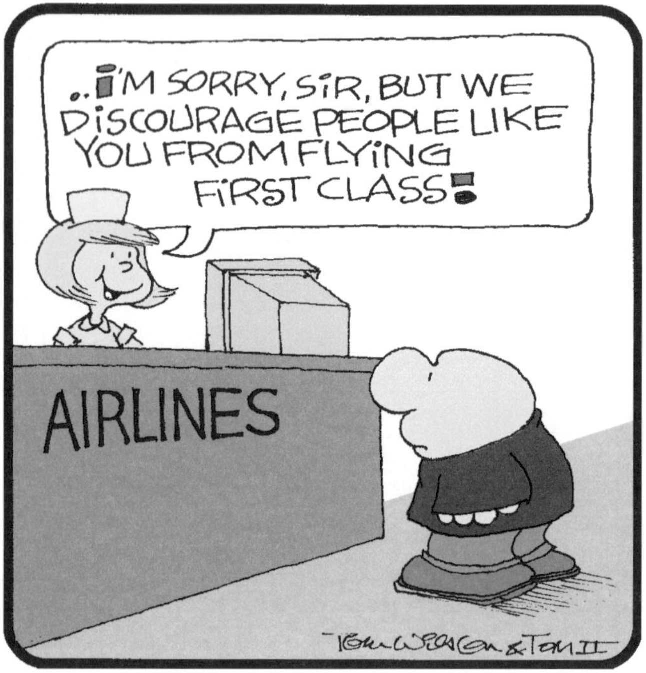
..I'M SORRY, SIR, BUT WE DISCOURAGE PEOPLE LIKE YOU FROM FLYING FIRST CLASS!
AIRLINES

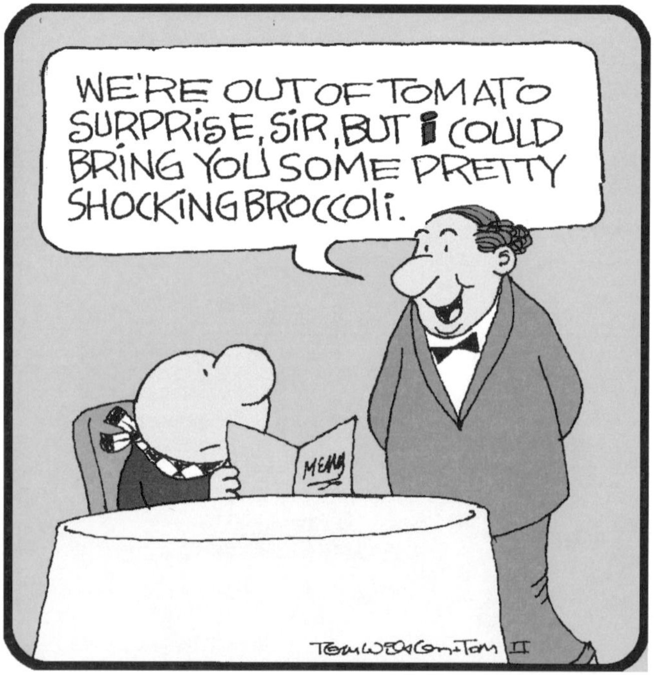
WE'RE OUT OF TOMATO SURPRISE, SIR, BUT I COULD BRING YOU SOME PRETTY SHOCKING BROCCOLI.
MENU

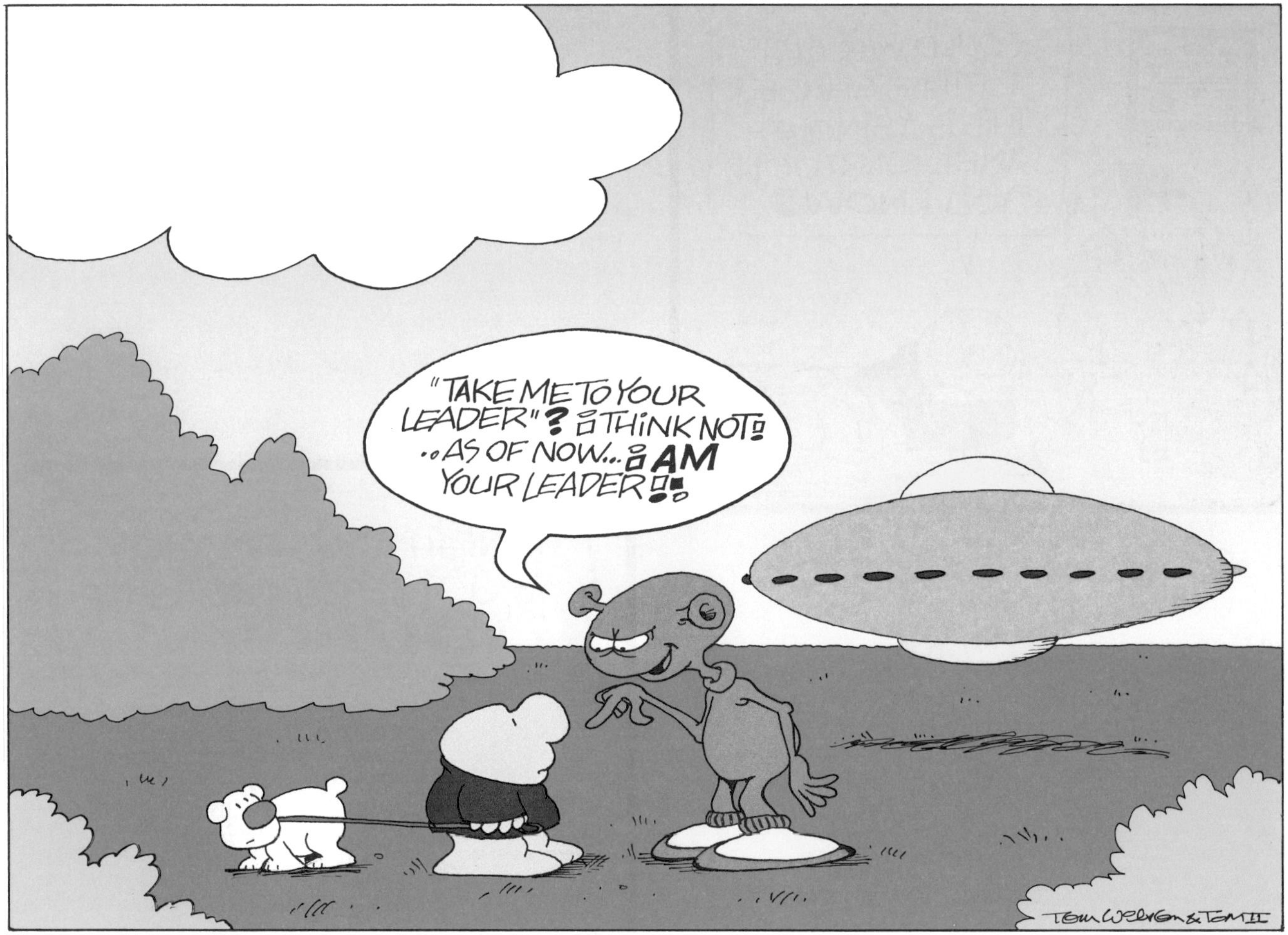
"TAKE ME TO YOUR LEADER"? I THINK NOT! ..AS OF NOW... I AM YOUR LEADER!!!

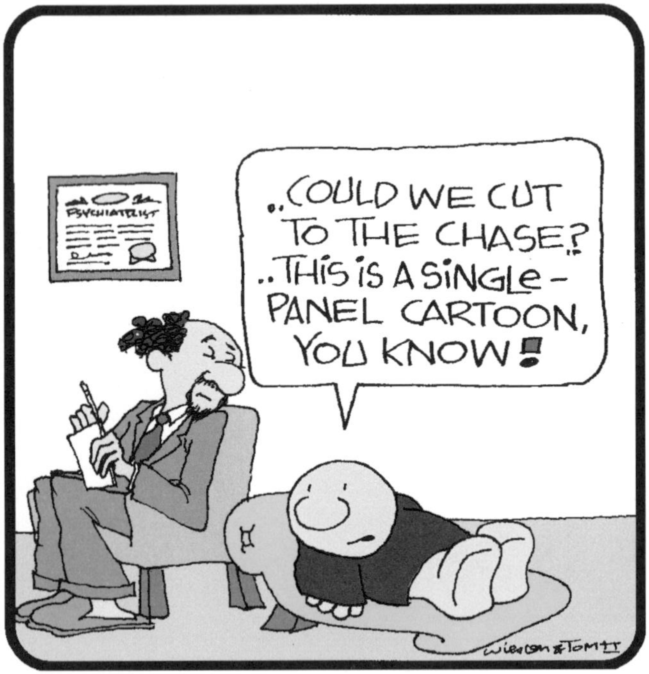
..COULD WE CUT TO THE CHASE? ..THIS IS A SINGLE-PANEL CARTOON, YOU KNOW!
PSYCHIATRIST

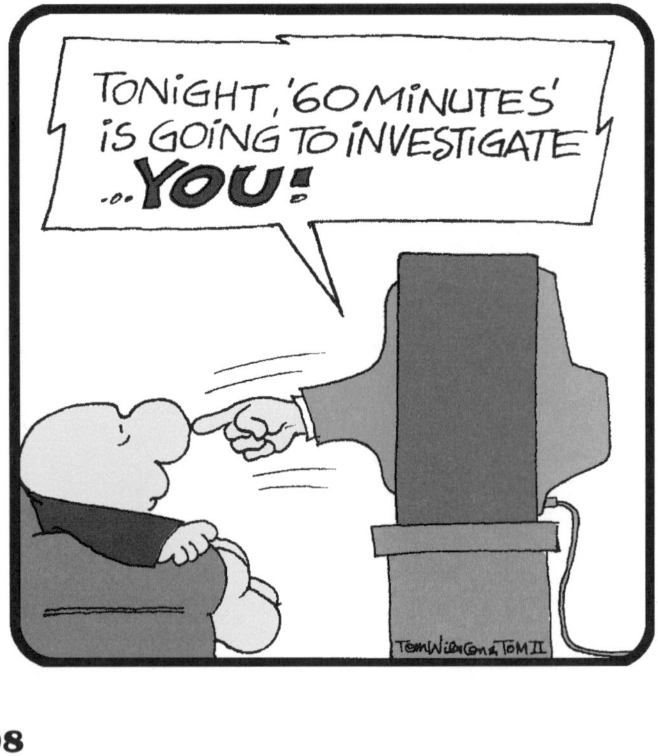
TONIGHT, '60 MINUTES' IS GOING TO INVESTIGATE ..o.. YOU!

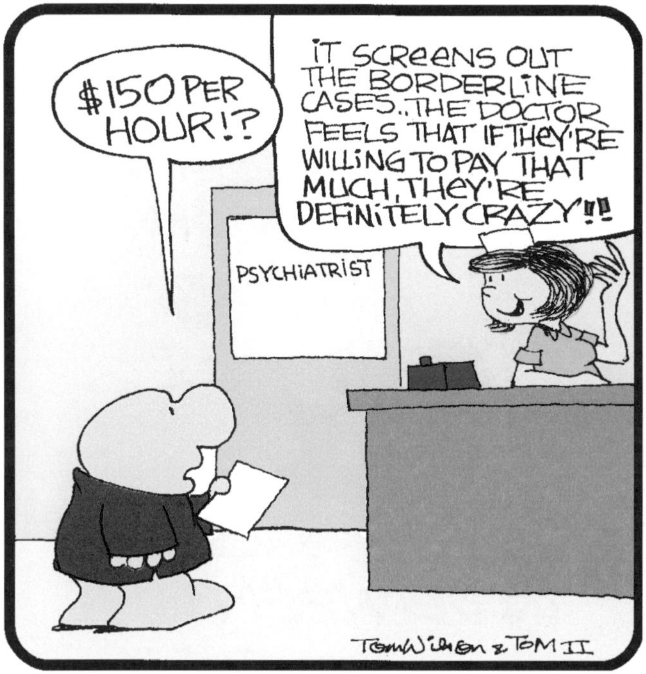
$150 PER HOUR!?
IT SCREENS OUT THE BORDERLINE CASES.. THE DOCTOR FEELS THAT IF THEY'RE WILLING TO PAY THAT MUCH, THEY'RE DEFINITELY CRAZY!!!
PSYCHIATRIST
Tom Wilson & Tom II

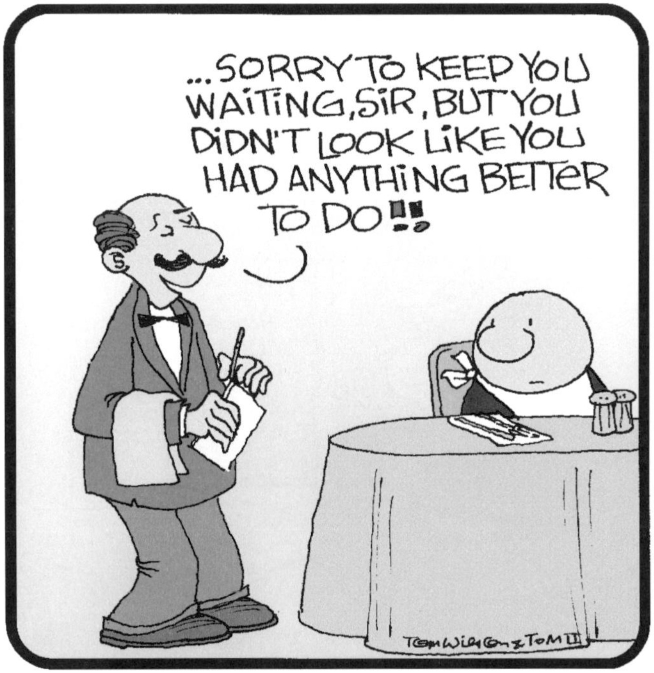
...SORRY TO KEEP YOU WAITING, SIR, BUT YOU DIDN'T LOOK LIKE YOU HAD ANYTHING BETTER TO DO!!!
Tom Wilson & Tom II

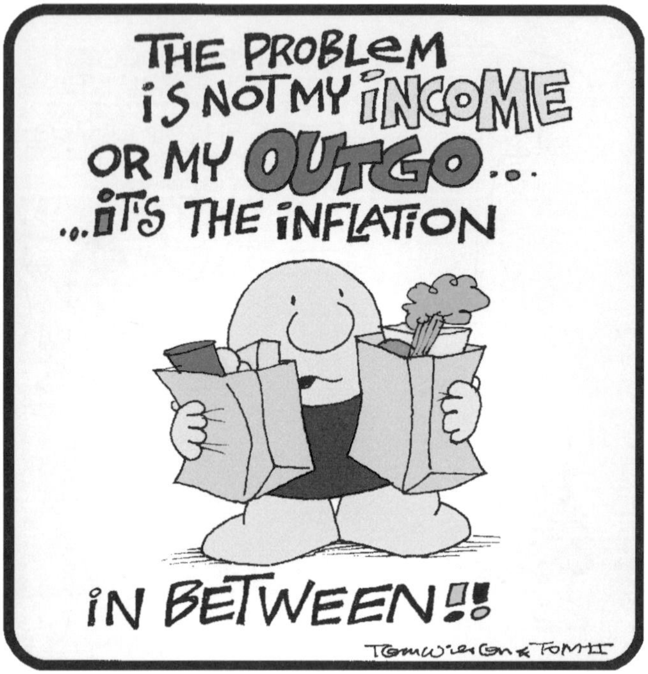
THE PROBLEM IS NOT MY INCOME OR MY OUTGO... ...IT'S THE INFLATION
IN BETWEEN!!
TOM WILSON & TOM II

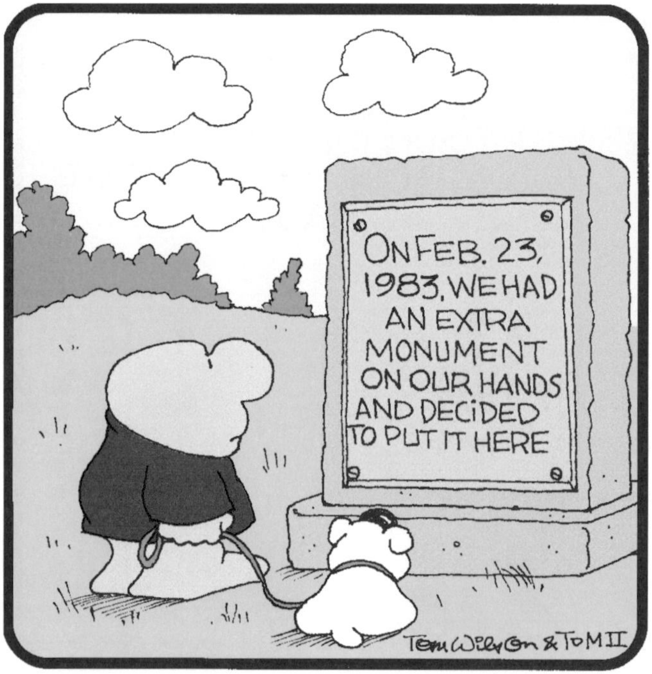
ON FEB. 23, 1983, WE HAD AN EXTRA MONUMENT ON OUR HANDS AND DECIDED TO PUT IT HERE
TOM WILSON & TOM II

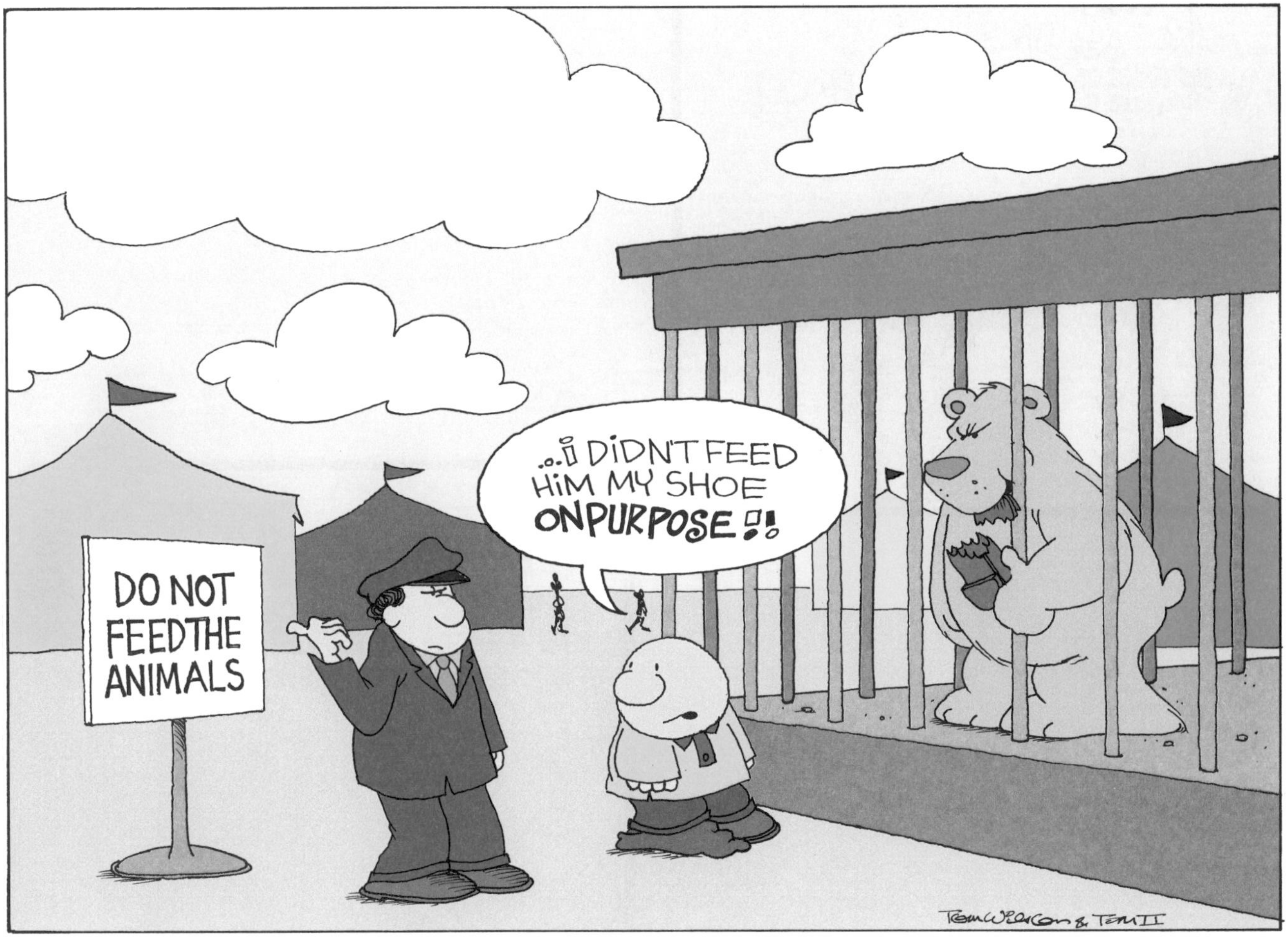
DO NOT FEED THE ANIMALS
...I DIDN'T FEED HIM MY SHOE ON PURPOSE!!
Tom Wilson & Tom II

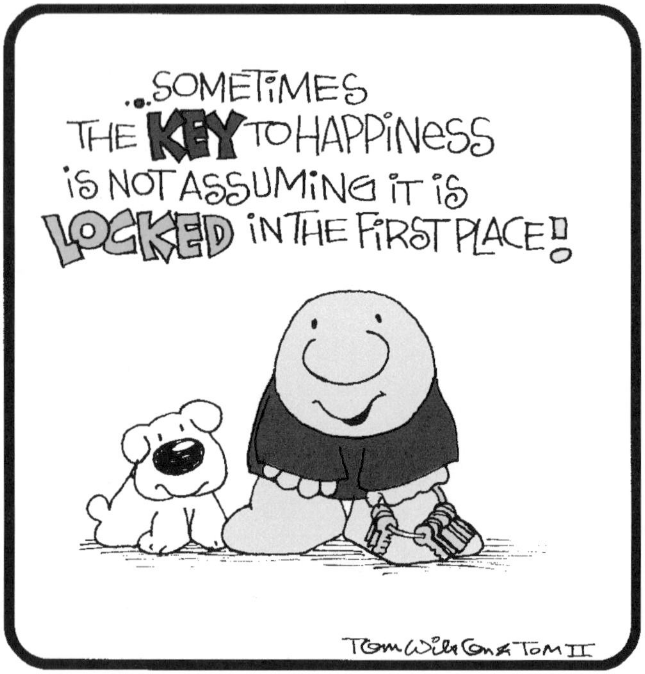
..SOMETIMES THE KEY TO HAPPINESS IS NOT ASSUMING IT IS LOCKED IN THE FIRST PLACE!
TOM WILSON & TOM II

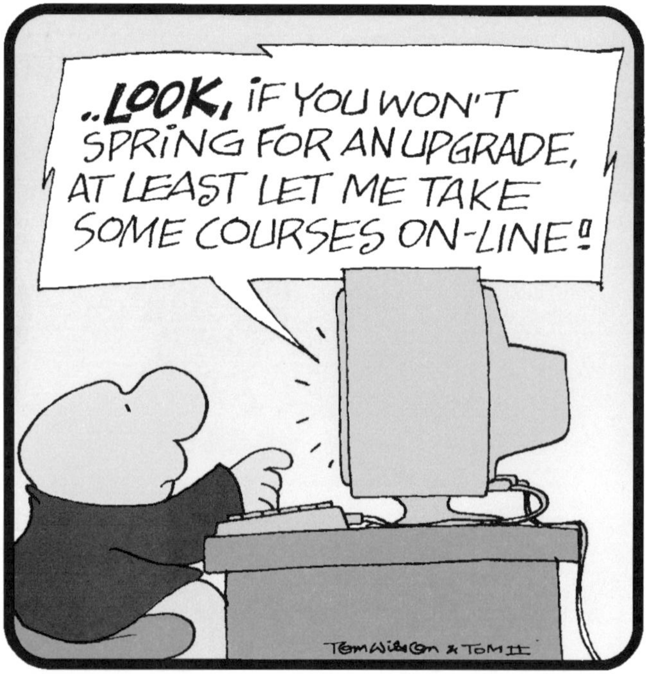
..LOOK, IF YOU WON'T SPRING FOR AN UPGRADE, AT LEAST LET ME TAKE SOME COURSES ON-LINE!
TOM WILSON & TOM II

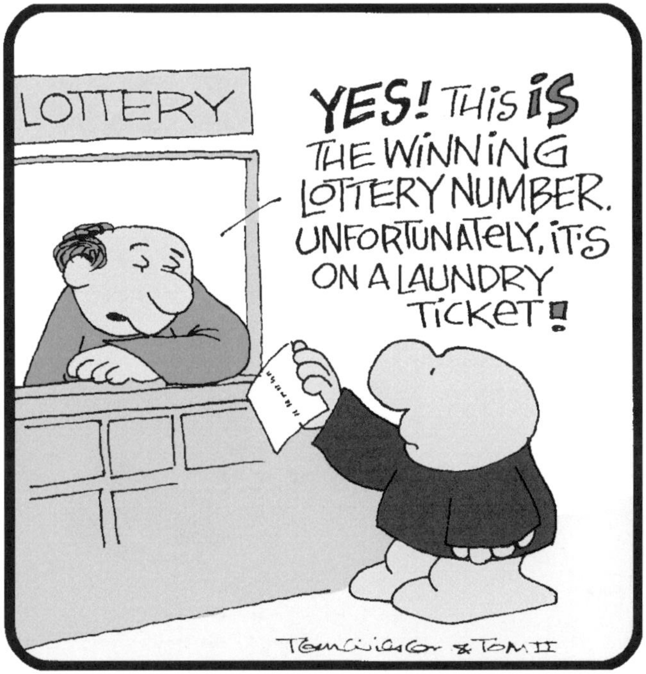
LOTTERY
YES! THIS IS THE WINNING LOTTERY NUMBER. UNFORTUNATELY, IT'S ON A LAUNDRY TICKET!
Tom Wilson & Tom II

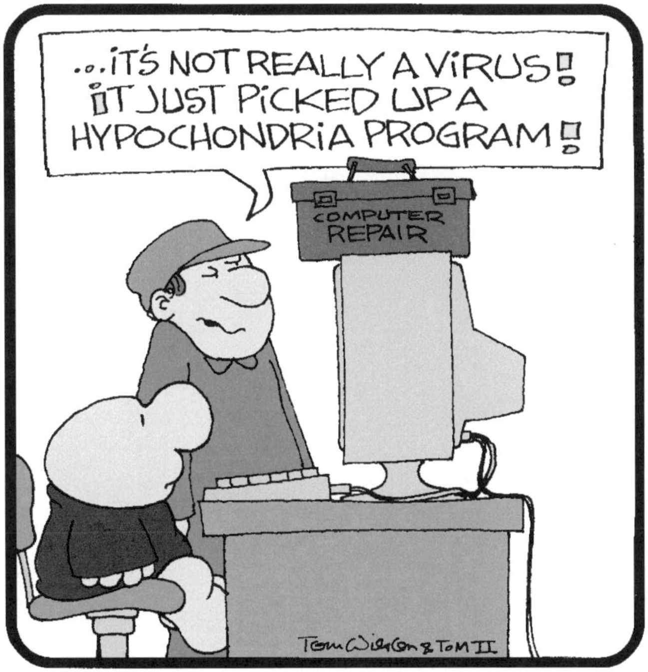
...IT'S NOT REALLY A VIRUS! IT JUST PICKED UP A HYPOCHONDRIA PROGRAM!
COMPUTER REPAIR
Tom Wilson & Tom II

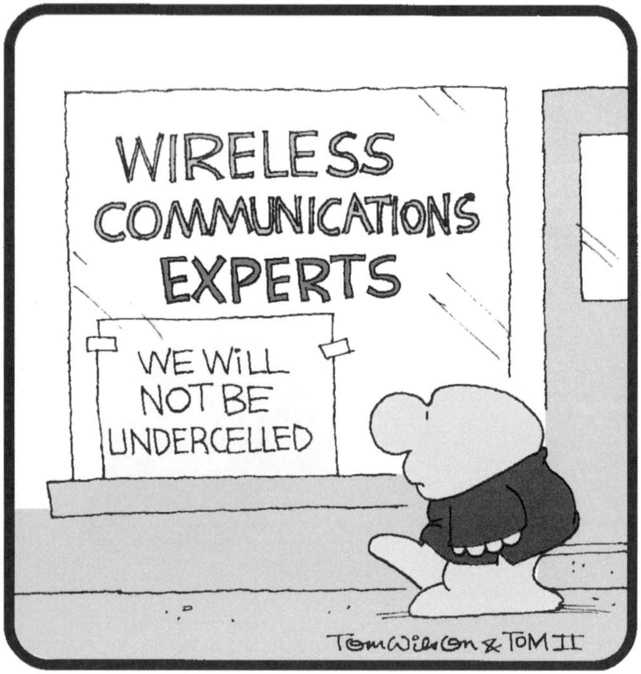
WIRELESS
COMMUNICATIONS
EXPERTS
WE WILL
NOT BE
UNDERCELLED

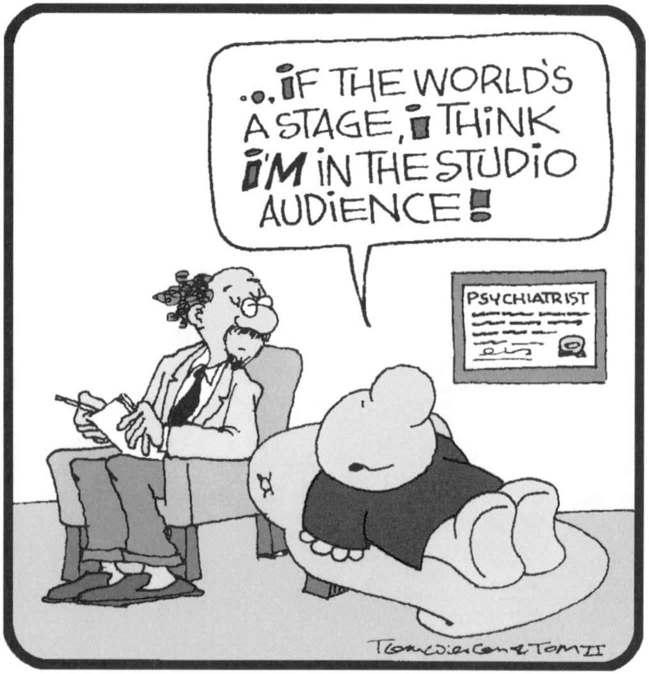
...IF THE WORLD'S A STAGE, I THINK I'M IN THE STUDIO AUDIENCE!
PSYCHIATRIST

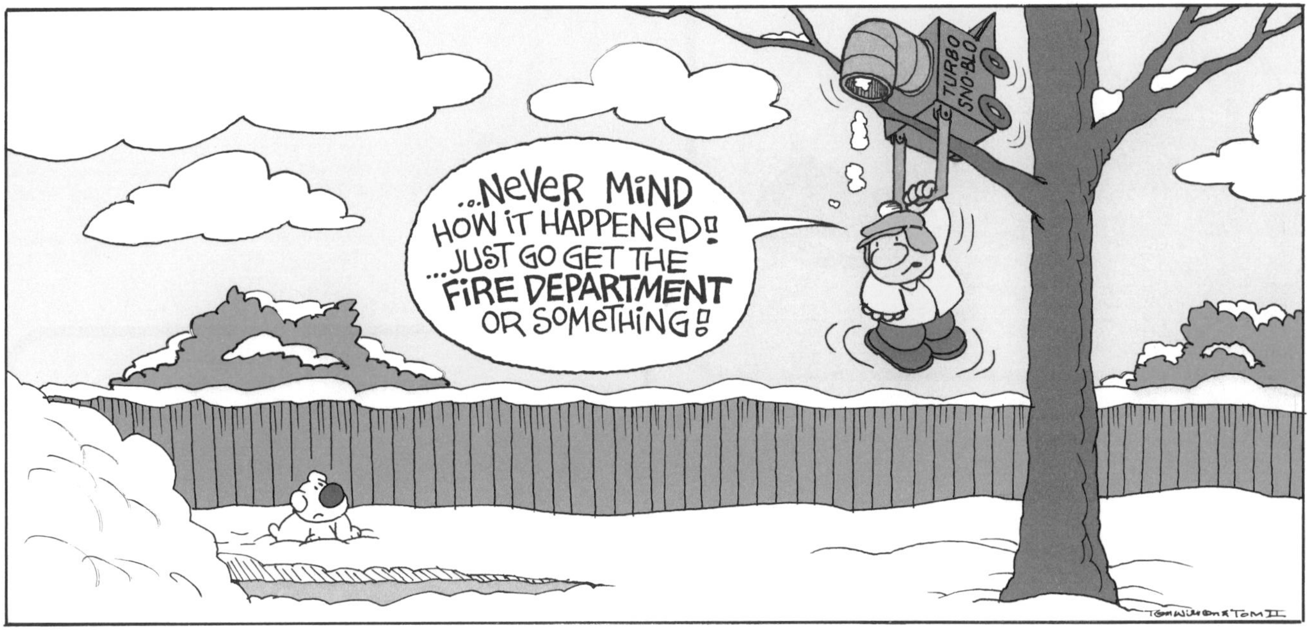
TURBO SNO-BLO
...NEVER MIND HOW IT HAPPENED! ...JUST GO GET THE FIRE DEPARTMENT OR SOMETHING!
TOM WILSON & TOM II

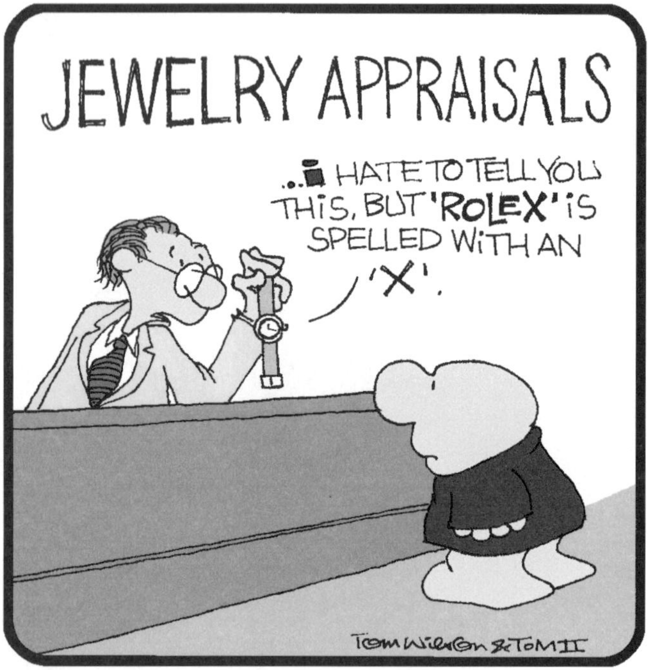
JEWELRY APPRAISALS
...I HATE TO TELL YOU THIS, BUT 'ROLEX' IS SPELLED WITH AN 'X'.
Tom Wilson & Tom II

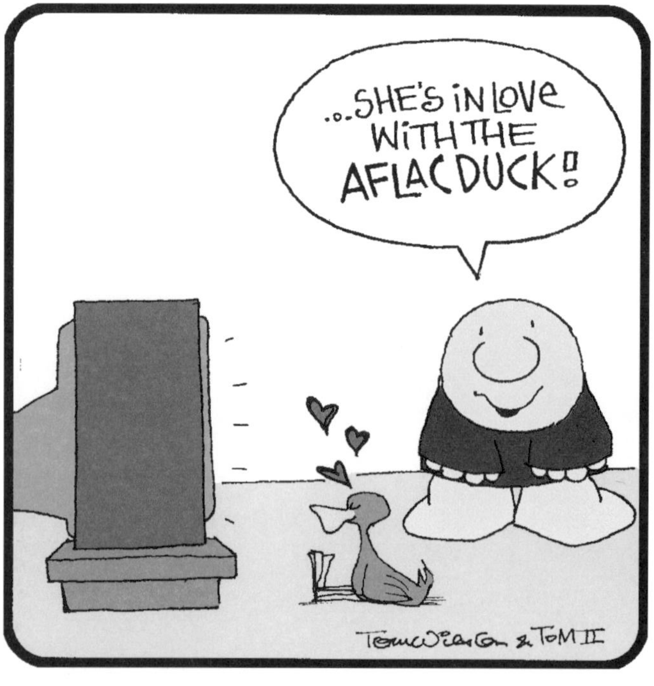
...SHE'S IN LOVE WITH THE AFLAC DUCK!
Tom Wilson & Tom II

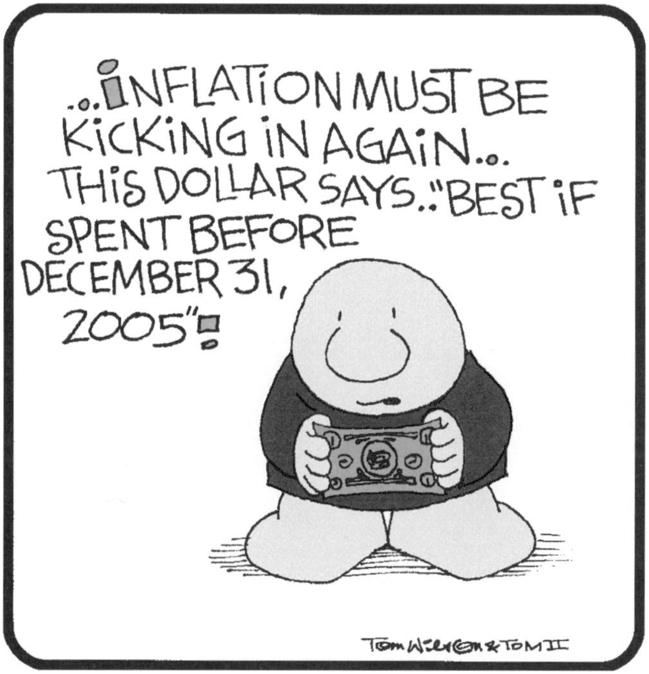
..INFLATION MUST BE KICKING IN AGAIN.. THIS DOLLAR SAYS.."BEST IF SPENT BEFORE DECEMBER 31, 2005"!
TOM WILSON & TOM II

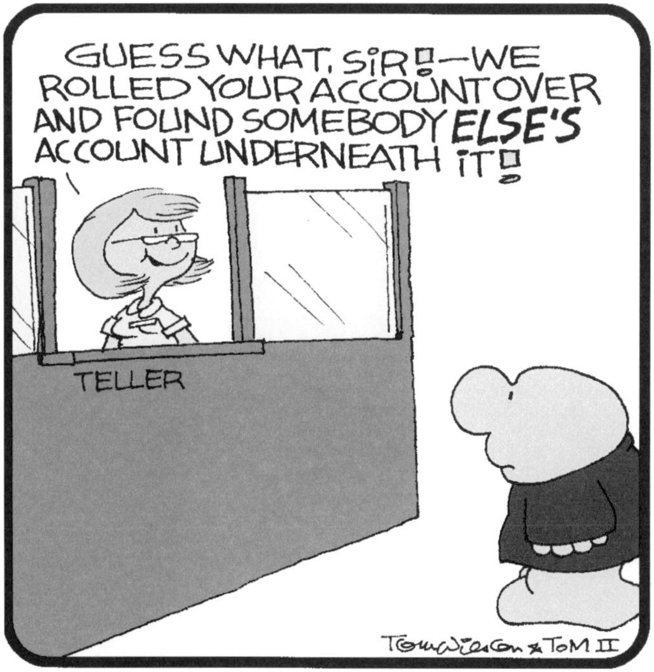
GUESS WHAT, SIR!—WE ROLLED YOUR ACCOUNT OVER AND FOUND SOMEBODY ELSE'S ACCOUNT UNDERNEATH IT!
TELLER
TOM WILSON & TOM II

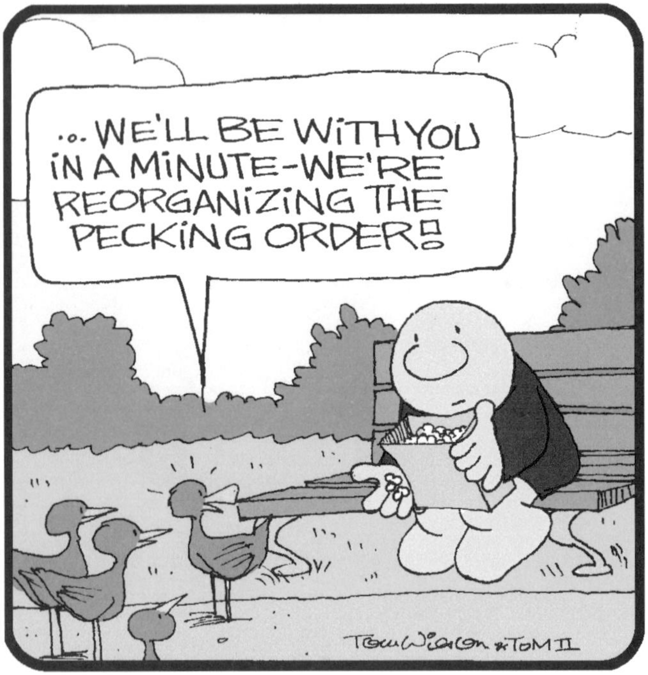
...WE'LL BE WITH YOU IN A MINUTE-WE'RE REORGANIZING THE PECKING ORDER!!

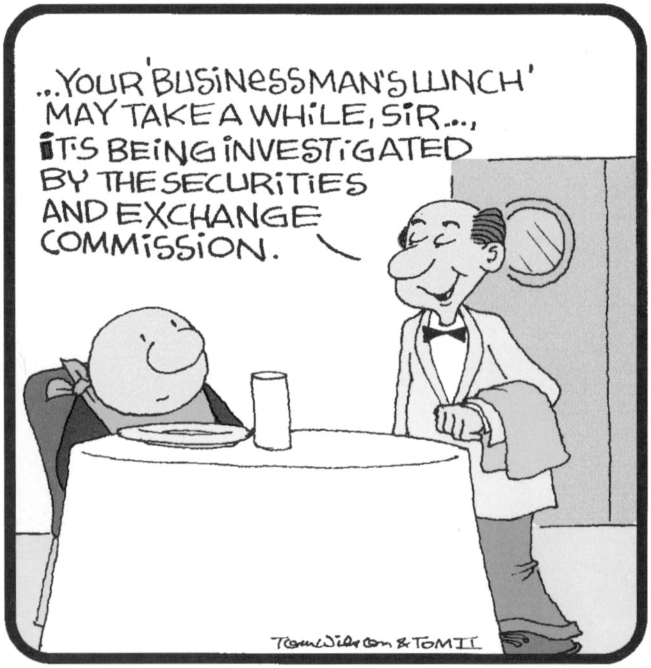
...YOUR 'BUSINESSMAN'S LUNCH' MAY TAKE A WHILE, SIR..., IT'S BEING INVESTIGATED BY THE SECURITIES AND EXCHANGE COMMISSION.

Z
BANG
CLANG
CRASH BASH BANG
BASH
KLAG
BANG
KLANG
HEY, PAL... iF YOU BOUGHT PLASTIC GARBAGE CANS...WE WOULDN'T WAKE YOU UP LIKE THIS!!
KACHUNG
CLANG

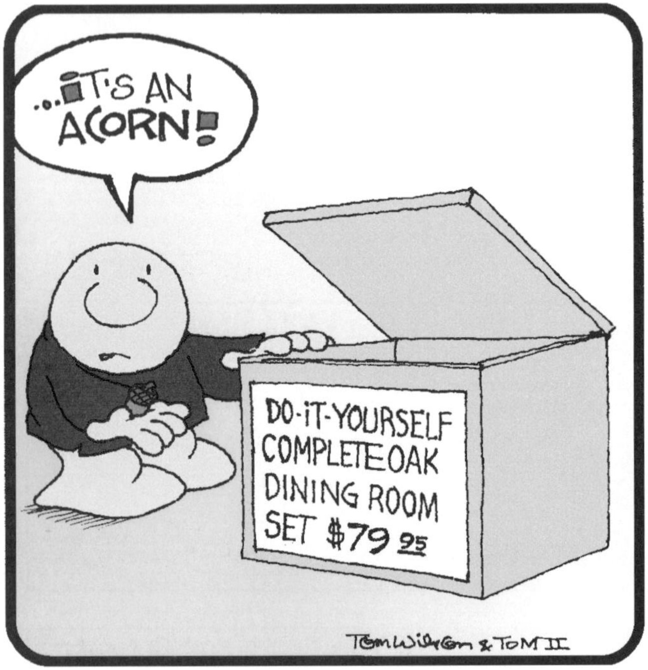
..IT'S AN ACORN!
DO-IT-YOURSELF COMPLETE OAK DINING ROOM SET $79 95
Tom Wilson & Tom II

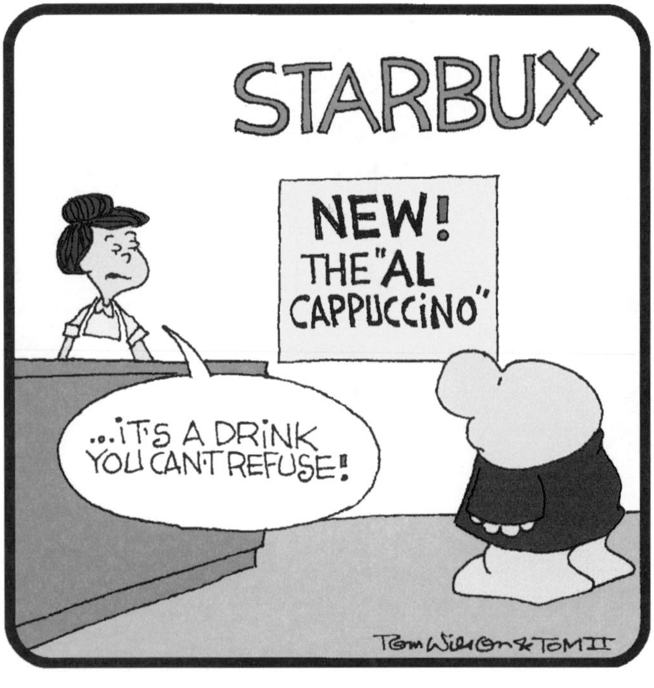
STARBUX
NEW! THE "AL CAPPUCCINO"
..IT'S A DRINK YOU CAN'T REFUSE!
Tom Wilson & Tom II

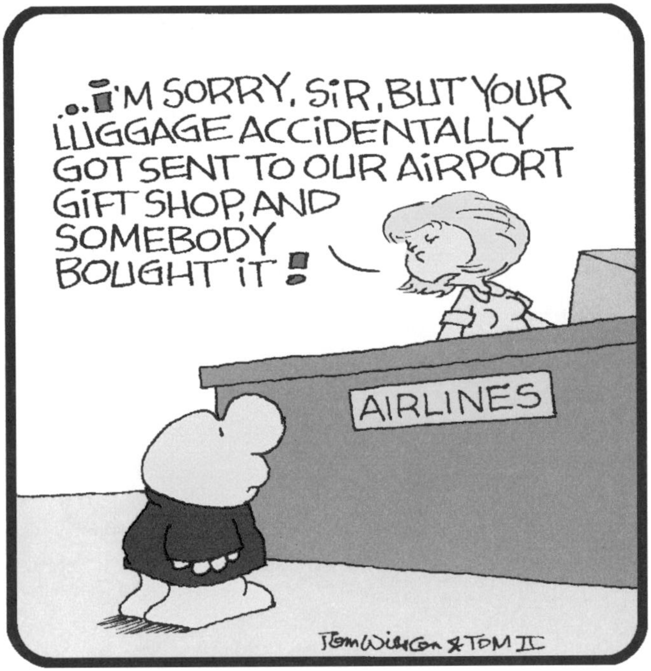
...I'M SORRY, SIR, BUT YOUR LUGGAGE ACCIDENTALLY GOT SENT TO OUR AIRPORT GIFT SHOP, AND SOMEBODY BOUGHT IT!
AIRLINES

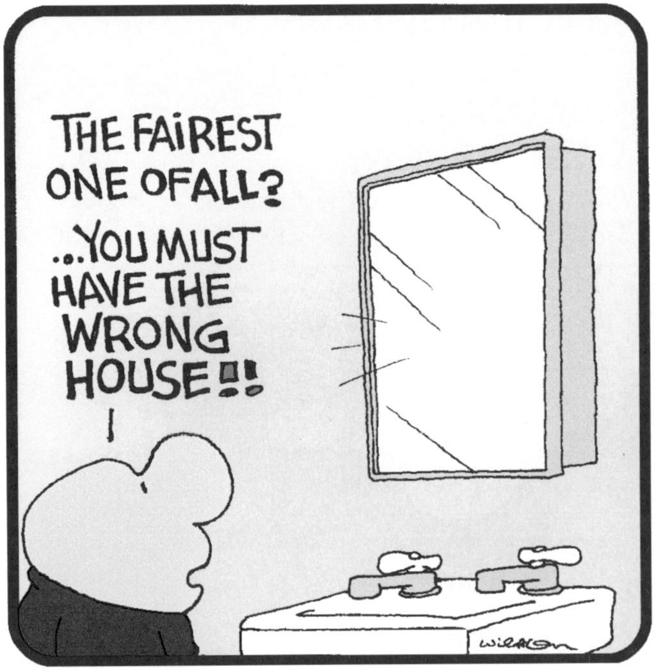
THE FAIREST ONE OF ALL?
...YOU MUST HAVE THE WRONG HOUSE!!

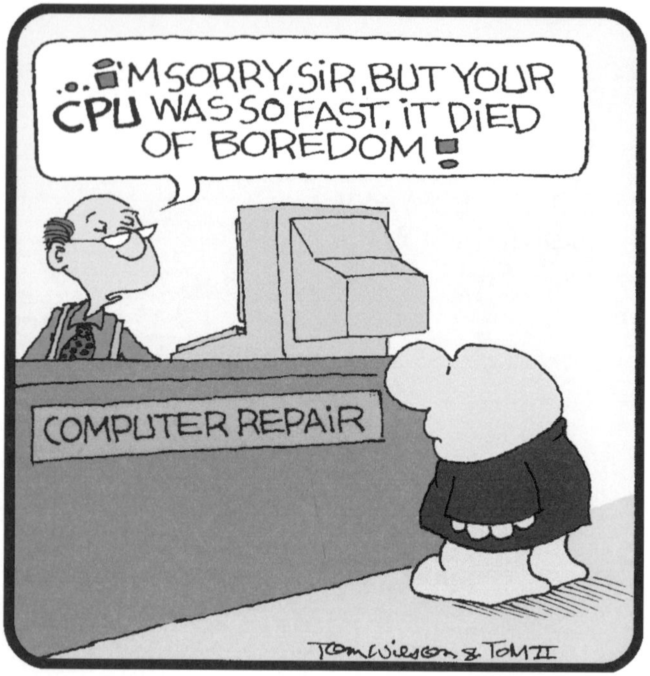
...I'M SORRY, SIR, BUT YOUR CPU WAS SO FAST, IT DIED OF BOREDOM!
COMPUTER REPAIR
TOM WILSON & TOM II

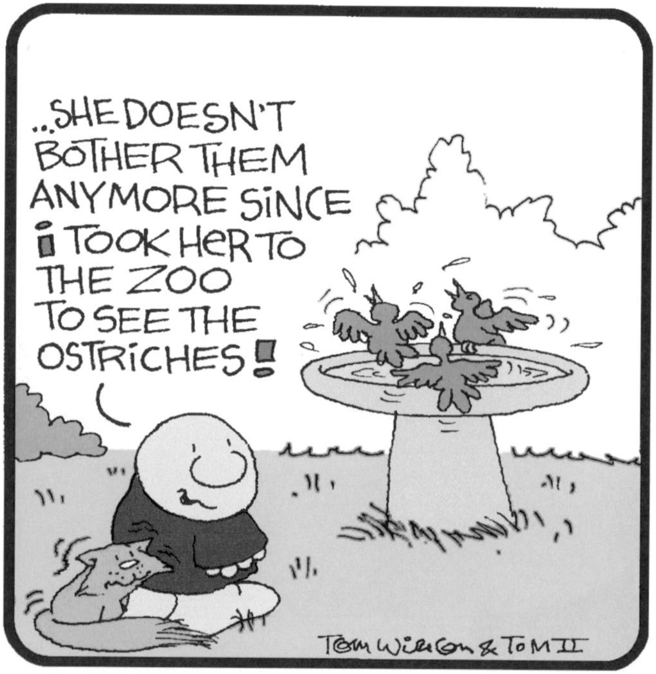
...SHE DOESN'T BOTHER THEM ANYMORE SINCE I TOOK HER TO THE ZOO TO SEE THE OSTRICHES!
TOM WILSON & TOM II

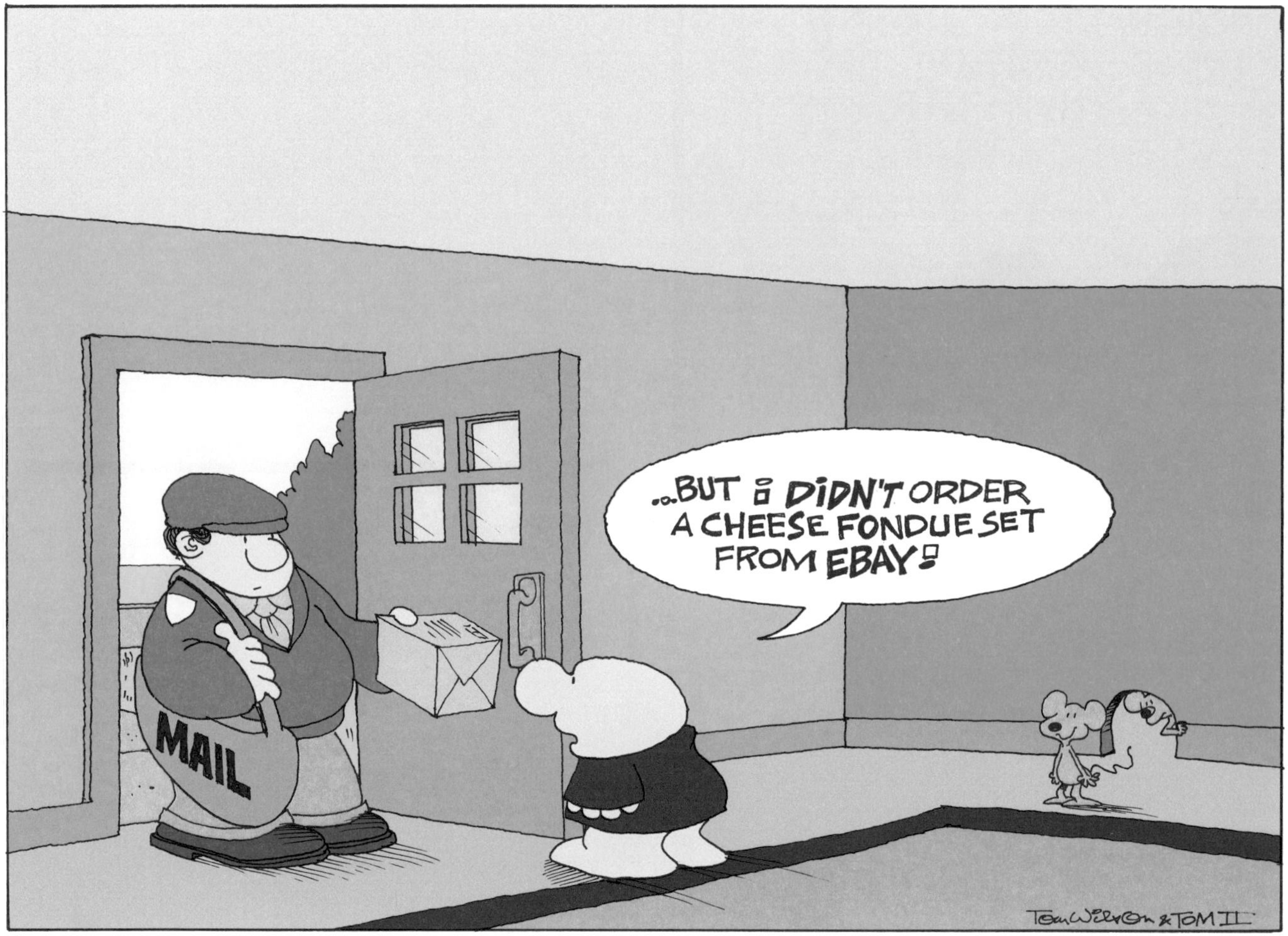
..BUT I DIDN'T ORDER A CHEESE FONDUE SET FROM EBAY!
MAIL
TomWilson &TOM II

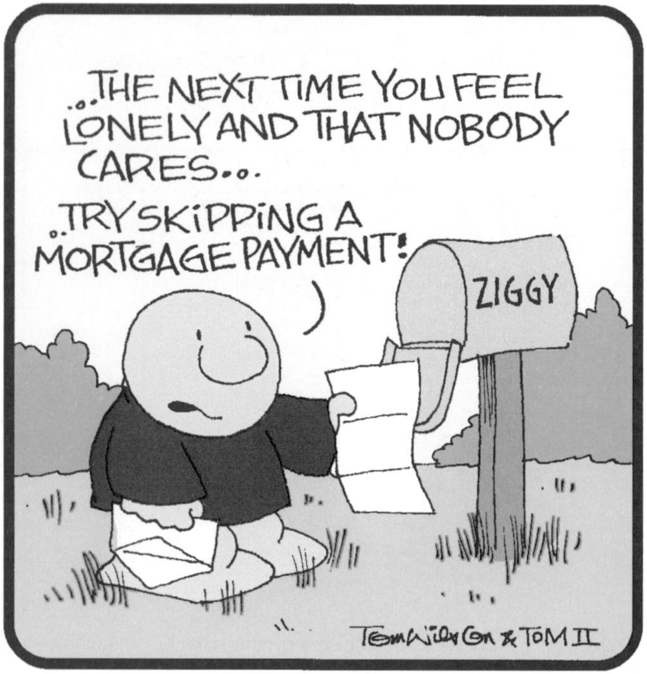
..THE NEXT TIME YOU FEEL LONELY AND THAT NOBODY CARES...
..TRY SKIPPING A MORTGAGE PAYMENT!
ZIGGY
TOM WILSON & TOM II

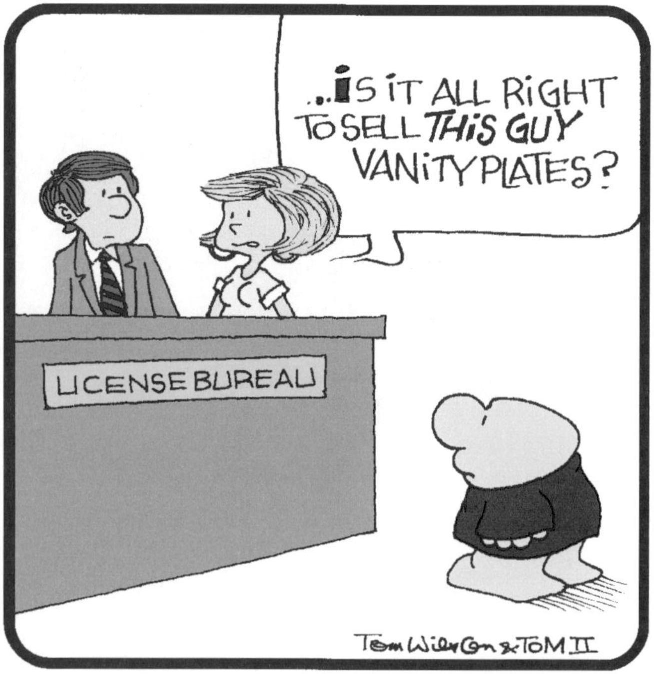
..IS IT ALL RIGHT TO SELL THIS GUY VANITY PLATES?
LICENSE BUREAU
TOM WILSON & TOM II

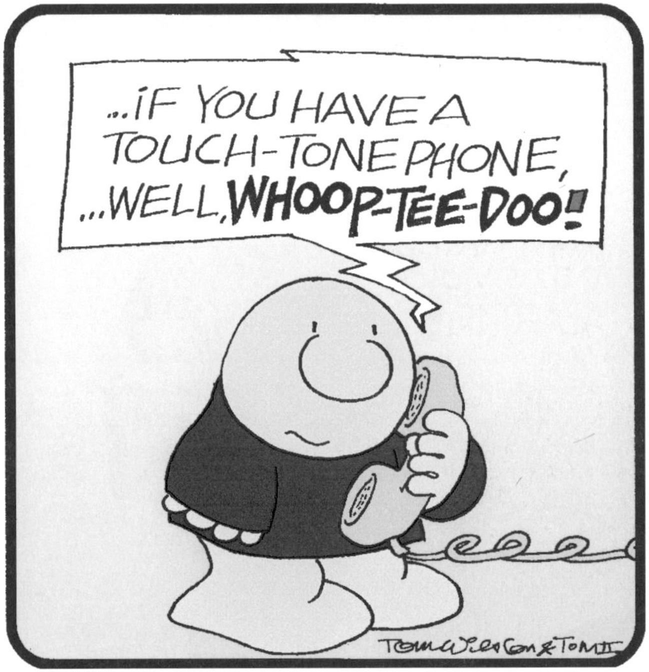
..IF YOU HAVE A TOUCH-TONE PHONE, ...WELL, WHOOP-TEE-DOO!
TOM WILSON & TOM II

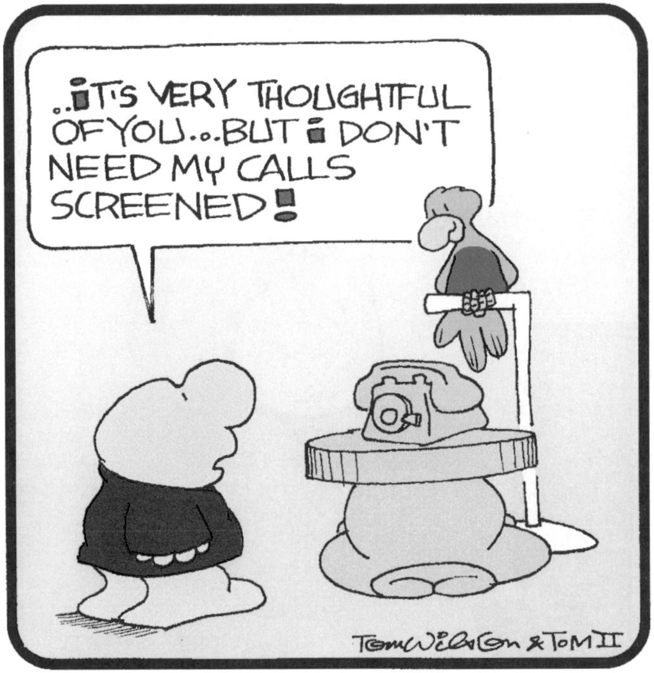
..IT'S VERY THOUGHTFUL OF YOU...BUT I DON'T NEED MY CALLS SCREENED!
TOM WILSON & TOM II

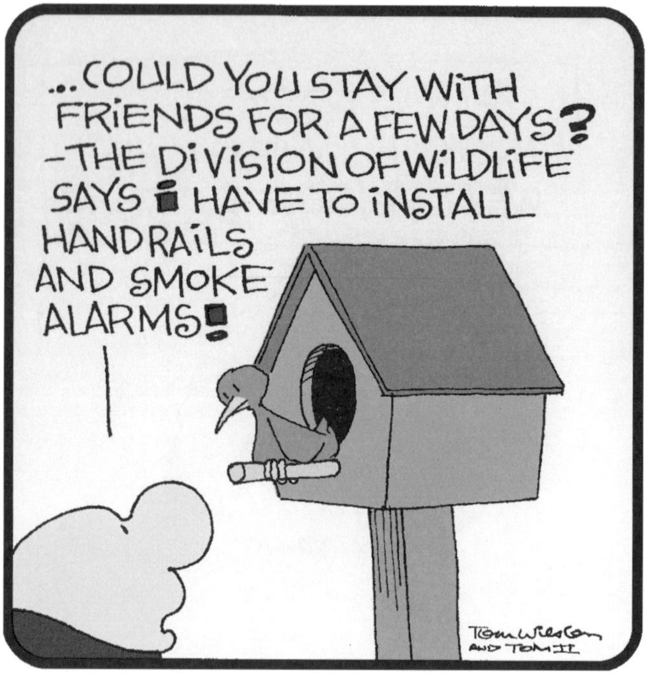
...COULD YOU STAY WITH FRIENDS FOR A FEW DAYS? -THE DIVISION OF WILDLIFE SAYS I HAVE TO INSTALL HANDRAILS AND SMOKE ALARMS!
TOM WILSON AND TOM II

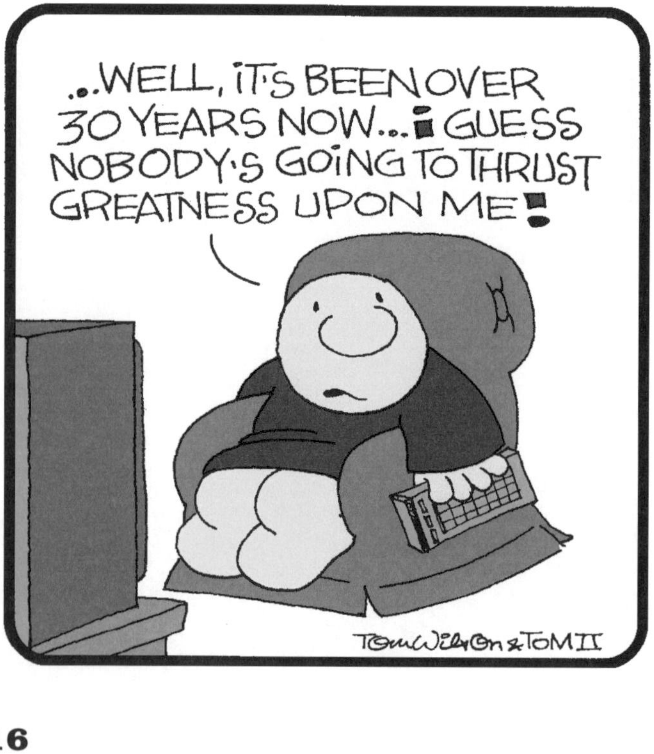
...WELL, IT'S BEEN OVER 30 YEARS NOW... I GUESS NOBODY'S GOING TO THRUST GREATNESS UPON ME!
TOM WILSON & TOM II

ZIGGY, THESE FEELINGS OF DISAPPOINTMENT, INADEQUACY, UNFULFILLMENT AND GUILT...
WISEMAN
ONE MUST SEE THESE AS HEALTHY REFLEXES,
..IN FACT, EVEN AS OPPORTUNITIES FOR POSITIVE CHANGE!
?
TO SIMPLY WALLOW WITHIN THESE FEELINGS ONLY NOURISHES THE SEEDS OF NEGATIVE SELF-ESTEEM...
FOR CENTURIES WISEMEN HAVE PONDERED THE HUMAN CONDITION..FOR YOU I HAVE BUT ONE BIT OF SIMPLE ADVICE!
?
GET OVER YOURSELF!
..ER.. THANK YOU.

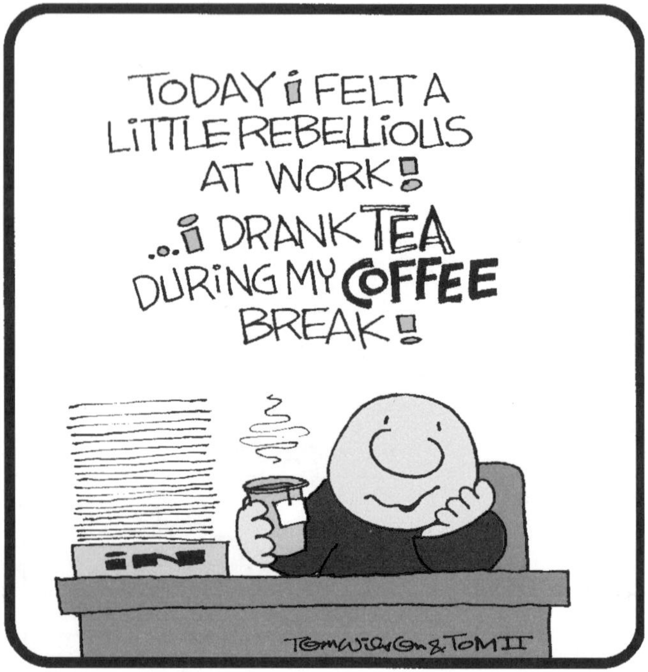
TODAY I FELT A LITTLE REBELLIOUS AT WORK!
..I DRANK TEA DURING MY COFFEE BREAK!
TOM WILSON & TOM II

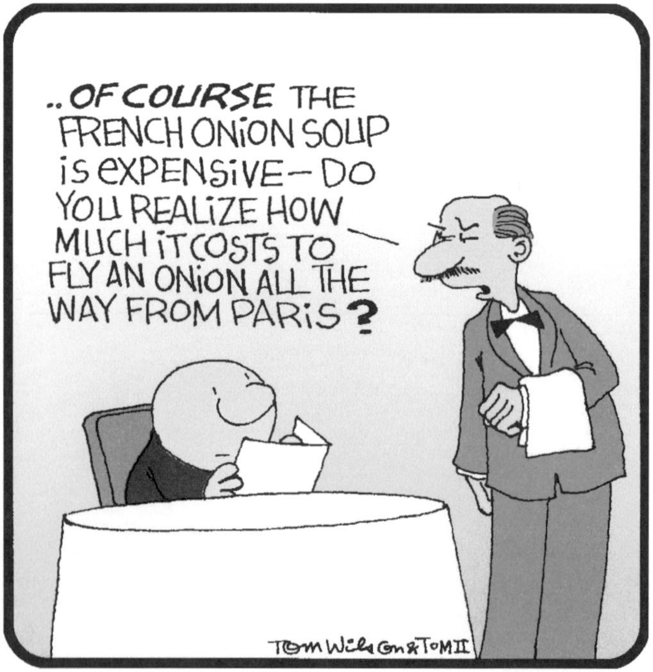
..OF COURSE THE FRENCH ONION SOUP IS EXPENSIVE – DO YOU REALIZE HOW MUCH IT COSTS TO FLY AN ONION ALL THE WAY FROM PARIS?
TOM WILSON & TOM II

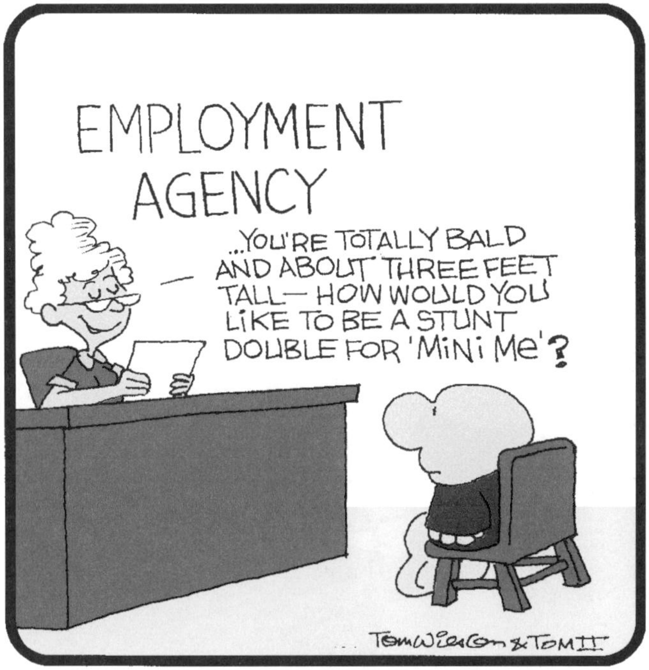
EMPLOYMENT AGENCY
...YOU'RE TOTALLY BALD AND ABOUT THREE FEET TALL— HOW WOULD YOU LIKE TO BE A STUNT DOUBLE FOR 'MINI ME'?
TOM WILSON & TOM II

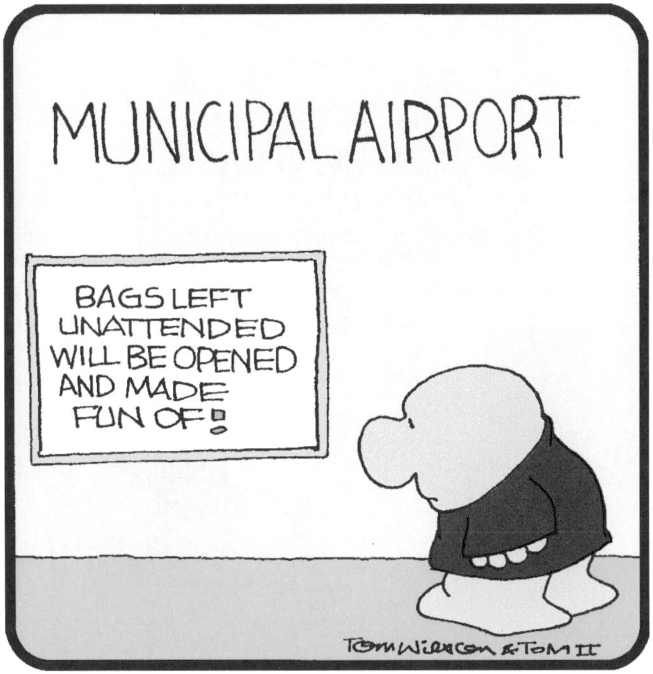
MUNICIPAL AIRPORT
BAGS LEFT UNATTENDED WILL BE OPENED AND MADE FUN OF!
TOM WILSON & TOM II

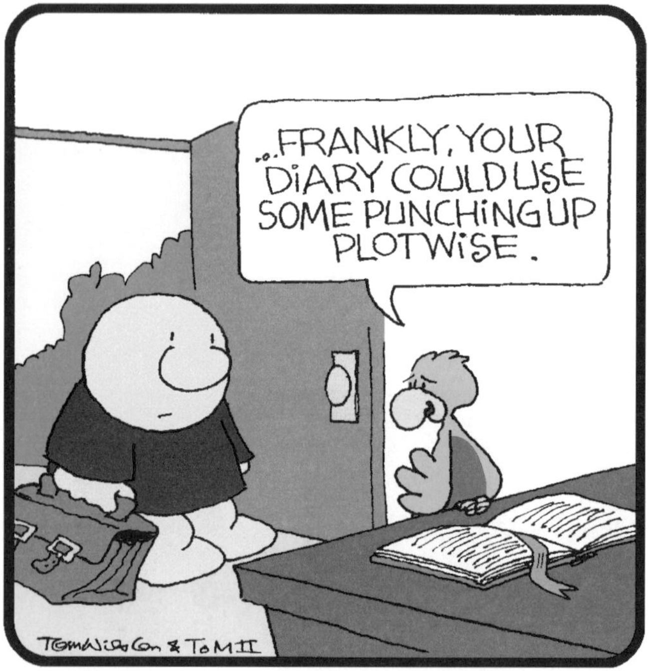
...FRANKLY, YOUR DIARY COULD USE SOME PUNCHING UP PLOTWISE.
TOM WILSON & TOM II

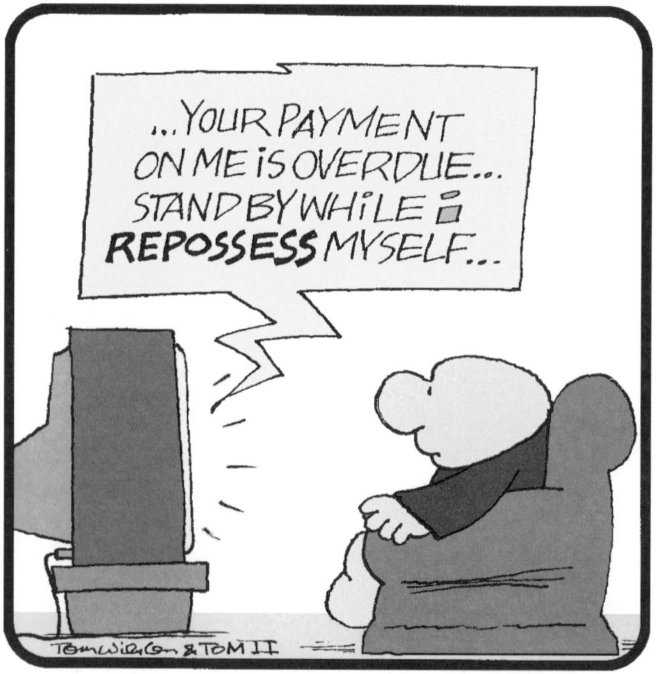
...YOUR PAYMENT ON ME IS OVERDUE... STAND BY WHILE I **REPOSSESS** MYSELF...
TOM WILSON & TOM II

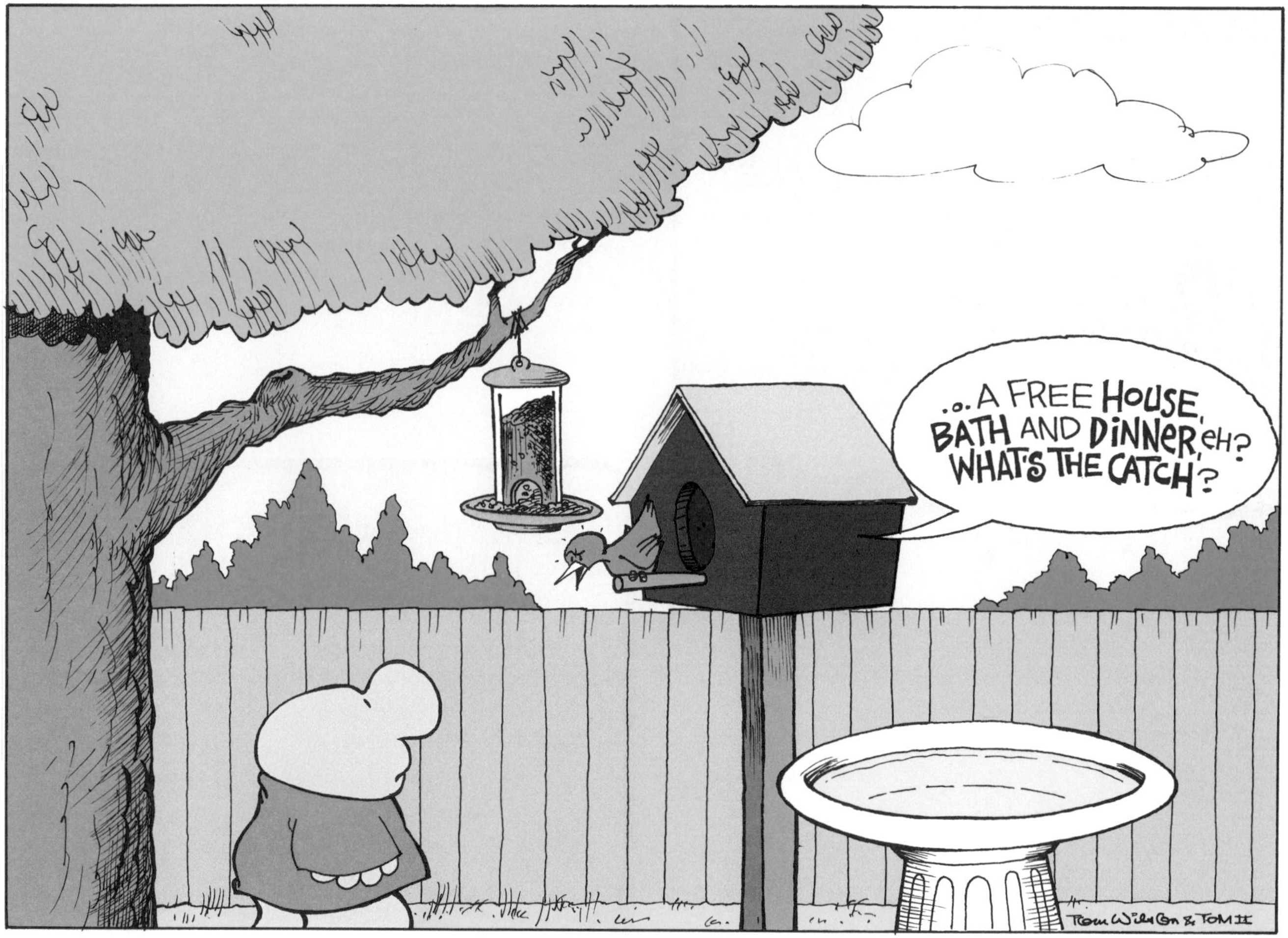
...A FREE HOUSE, BATH AND DINNER, EH? WHAT'S THE CATCH?
Tom Wilson & TOM II

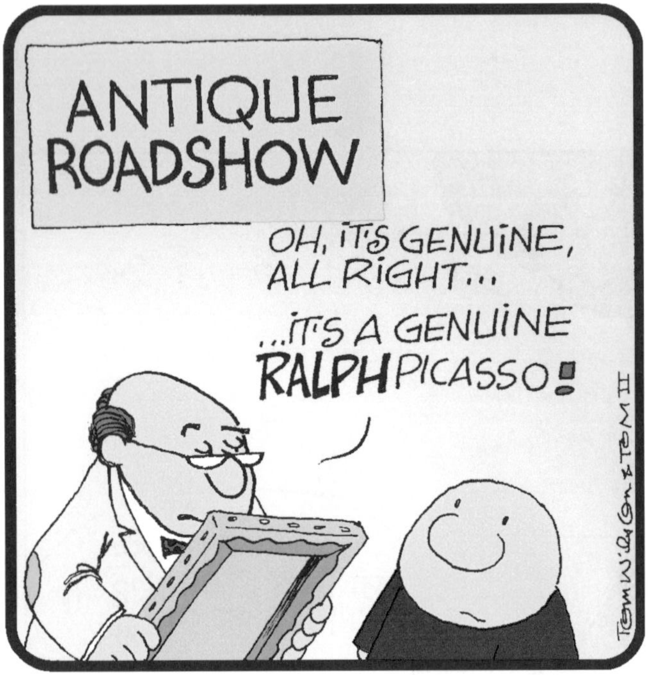
ANTIQUE ROADSHOW
OH, IT'S GENUINE, ALL RIGHT...
...IT'S A GENUINE RALPH PICASSO!
Tom Wilson & Tom II

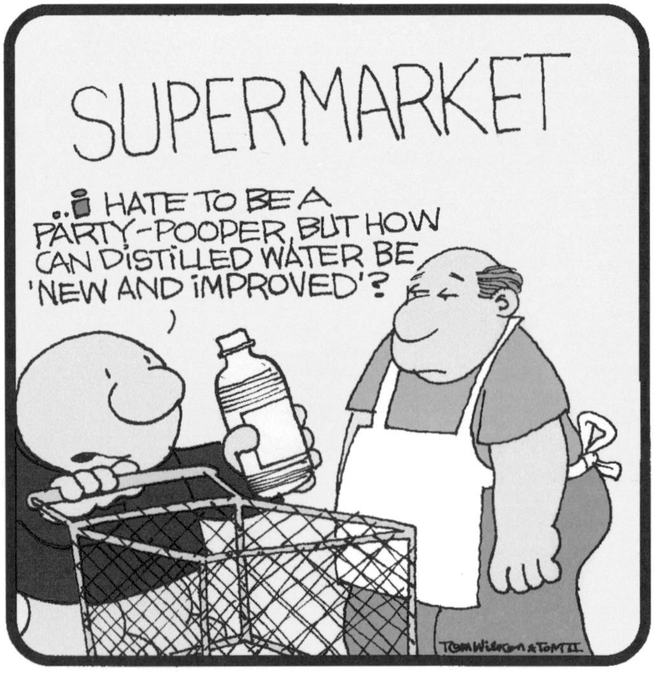
SUPERMARKET
..I HATE TO BE A PARTY-POOPER, BUT HOW CAN DISTILLED WATER BE 'NEW AND IMPROVED'?
Tom Wilson & Tom II

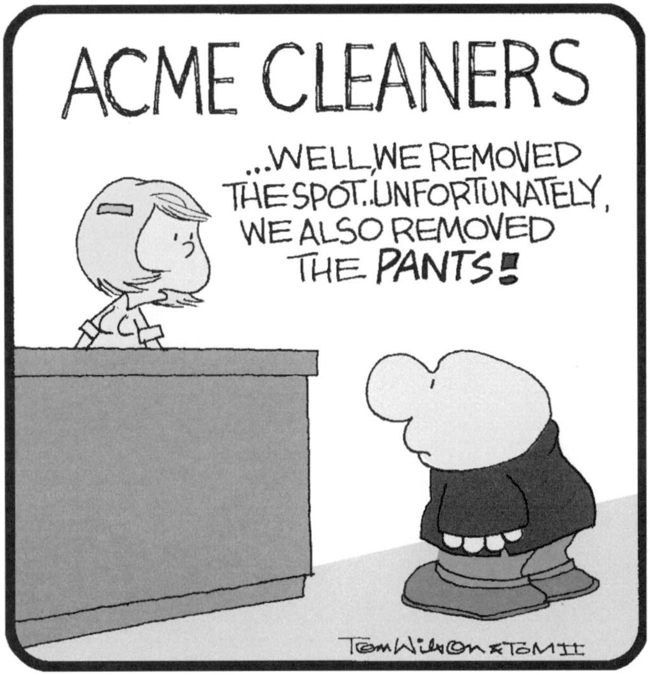
ACME CLEANERS
...WELL, WE REMOVED THE SPOT...UNFORTUNATELY, WE ALSO REMOVED THE PANTS!
TomWilson & TomII

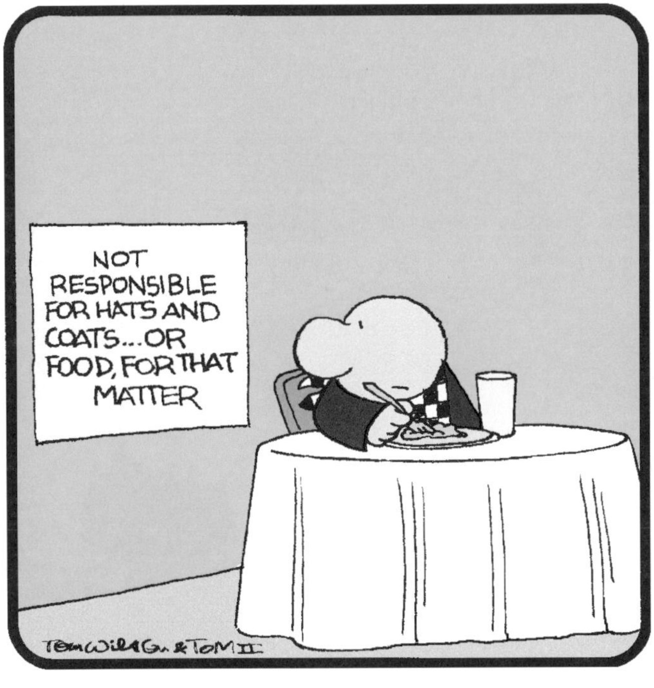
NOT RESPONSIBLE FOR HATS AND COATS...OR FOOD, FOR THAT MATTER
TomWilson & TomII

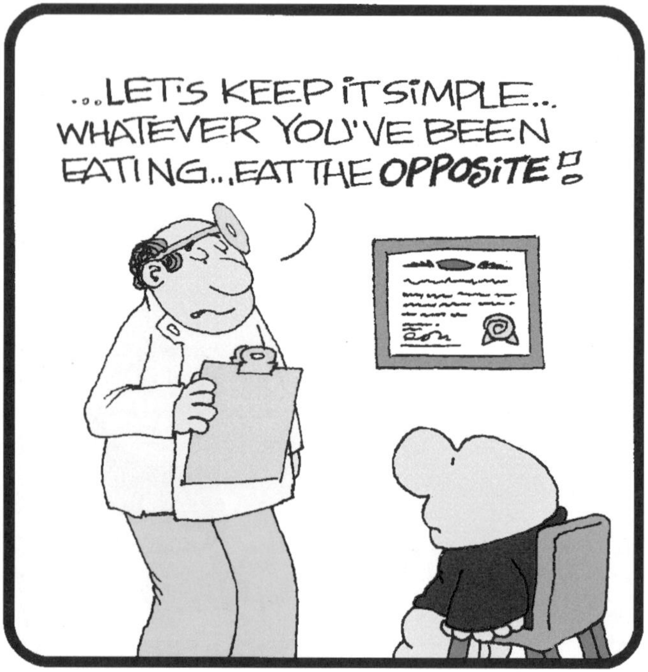
...LET'S KEEP IT SIMPLE... WHATEVER YOU'VE BEEN EATING...EAT THE OPPOSITE!!

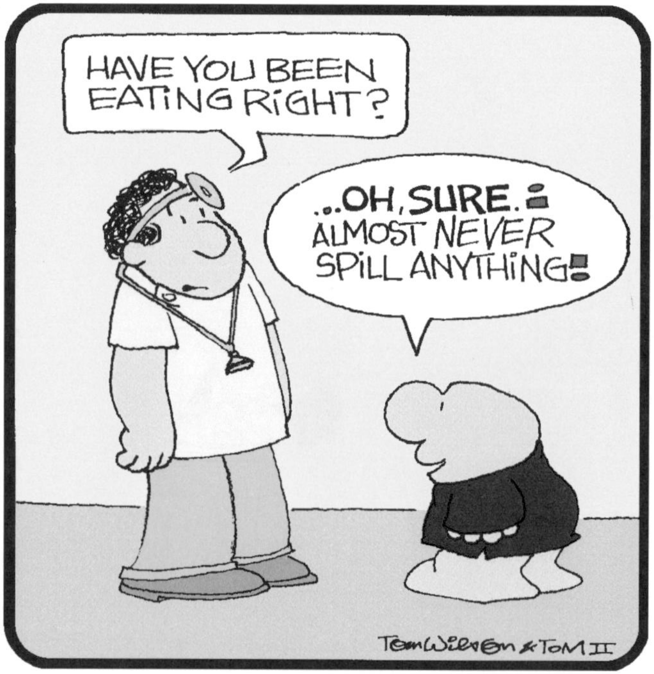
HAVE YOU BEEN EATING RIGHT?
...OH, SURE..! ALMOST NEVER SPILL ANYTHING!!
Tom Wilson & Tom II

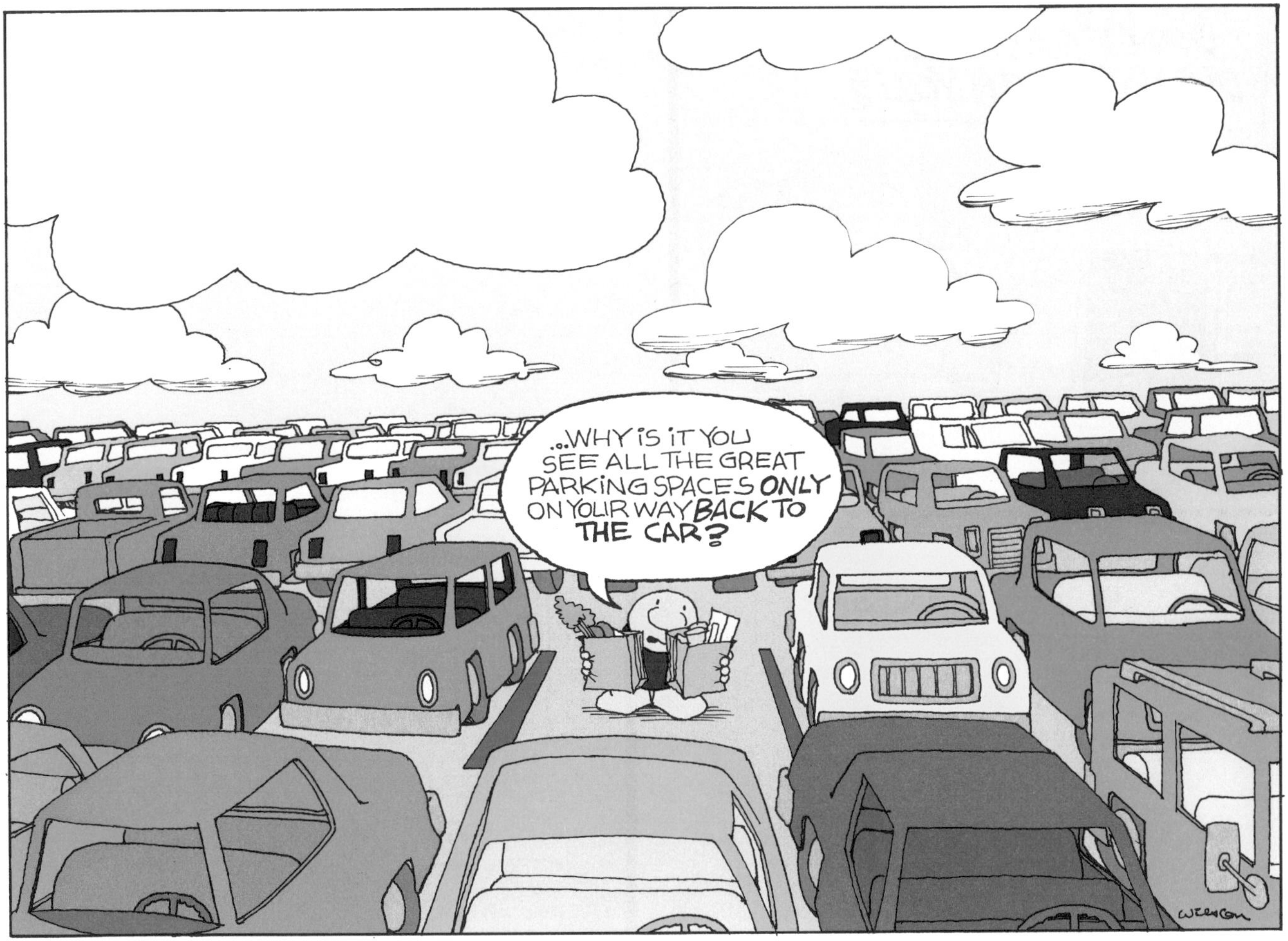
...WHY IS IT YOU SEE ALL THE GREAT PARKING SPACES ONLY ON YOUR WAY BACK TO THE CAR?

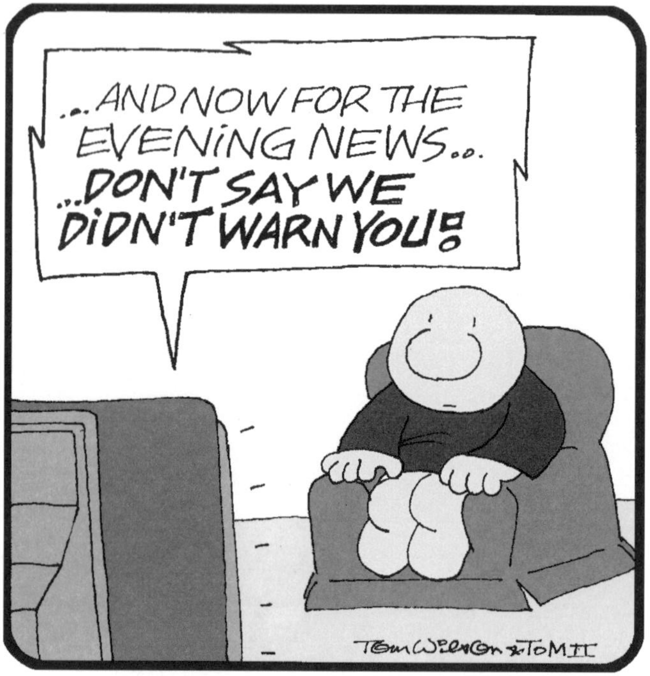
...AND NOW FOR THE EVENING NEWS... ...DON'T SAY WE DIDN'T WARN YOU!
TOM WILSON & TOM II

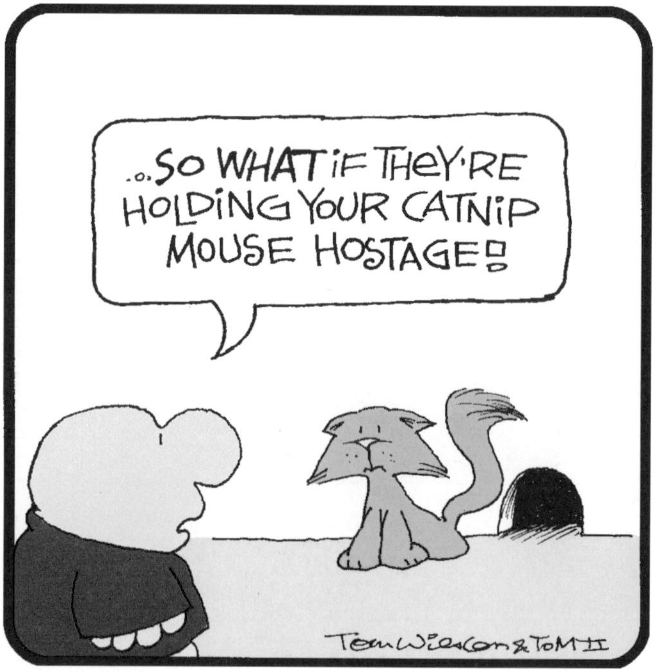
...SO WHAT IF THEY'RE HOLDING YOUR CATNIP MOUSE HOSTAGE!
TOM WILSON & TOM II

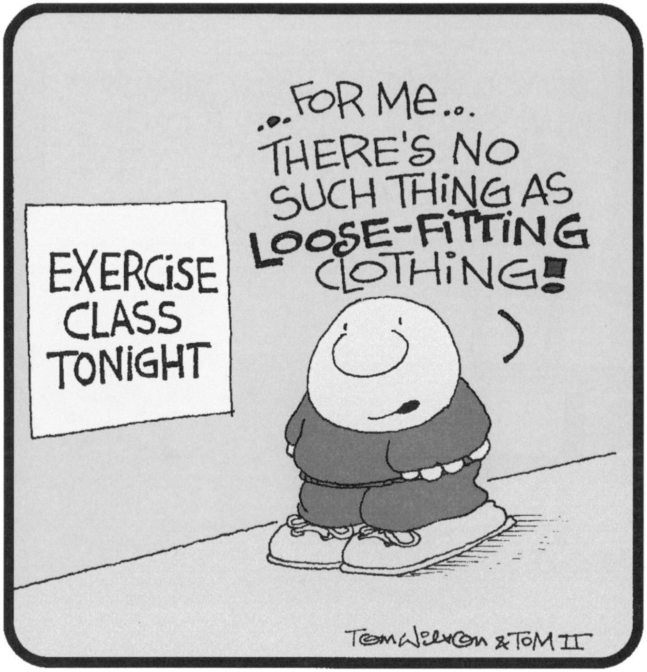
...FOR ME...
THERE'S NO SUCH THING AS LOOSE-FITTING CLOTHING!
EXERCISE CLASS TONIGHT
TOM WILSON & TOM II

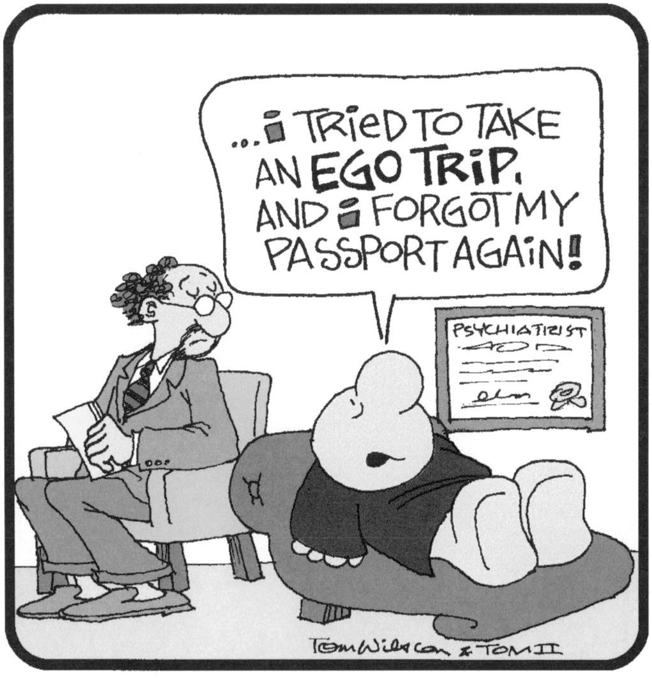
...I TRIED TO TAKE AN EGO TRIP, AND I FORGOT MY PASSPORT AGAIN!
PSYCHIATRIST
TOM WILSON & TOM II

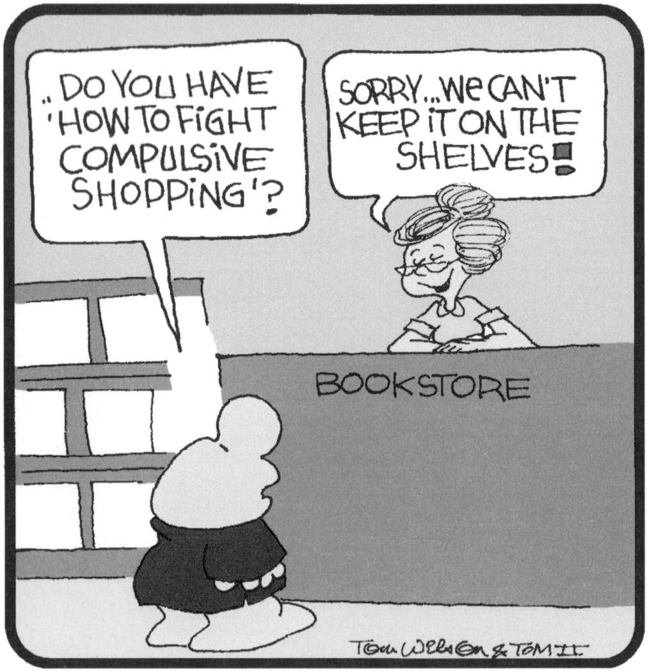
.. DO YOU HAVE 'HOW TO FIGHT COMPULSIVE SHOPPING'?
SORRY... WE CAN'T KEEP IT ON THE SHELVES!
BOOKSTORE
TOM WILSON & TOM II

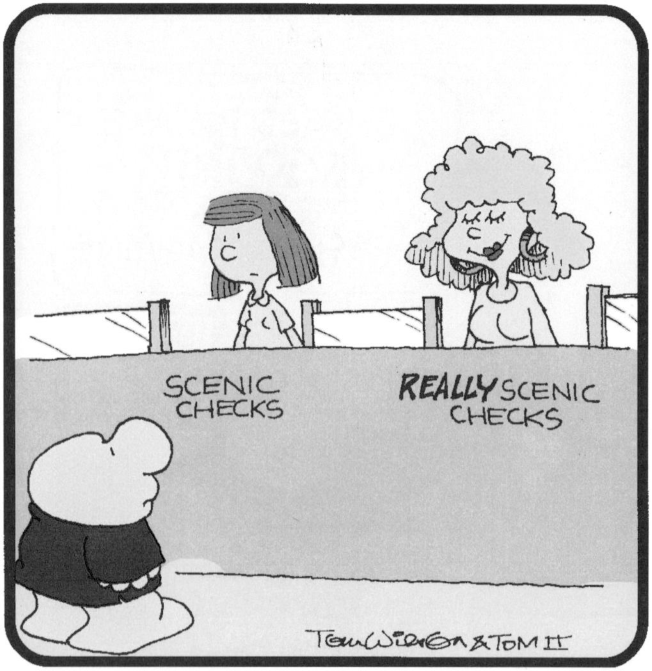
SCENIC CHECKS
REALLY SCENIC CHECKS
TOM WILSON & TOM II